LIFE IN THE BALANCE

EXPLORING THE ABORTION CONTROVERSY

Robert N. Wennberg

GRAND RAPIDS, MICHIGAN

WILLIAM B. EERDMANS PUBLISHING COMPANY

Copyright ©1985 by Wm. B. Eerdmans Publishing Co.
255 Jefferson Ave. S.E., Grand Rapids, Mich. 49503
All rights reserved
Printed in the United States of America

Reprinted, April 1990

Library of Congress Cataloging in Publication Data

Wennberg, Robert N.
  Life in the balance.

  Bibliography: p.
  Includes index.
    1. Abortion—Moral and ethical aspects. 2. Abortion
—Religious aspects—Christianity. I. Title.
HQ767.15.W46 1985   363.4'6   85-16019

ISBN 0-8028-0061-0

Contents

v

Preface

This book is an attempt at a systematic moral evaluation of a crucial contemporary problem. Few moral issues have preoccupied our minds and emotions as the abortion controversy has. It is not going to go away so we might as well begin to think through the matter carefully. Without question it is an important and controversial topic, and the literature, already enormous, continues to grow rapidly. If there is any justification for my adding to it, it is to be found in what I hope is the unique blend contained in these pages. For my own interests extend to philosophy as well as theology, to academic as well as popular arguments, and these interests are reflected in this book.

I have, first of all, attempted to interact with the significant contributions of moral philosophers. In the past fifteen years, philosophers have increasingly given their attention and considerable analytical skills to normative ethical issues, and as a result they have produced an impressive body of literature on a broad range of moral questions, including abortion. The work of professional philosophers constitutes not merely *an* important resource but perhaps *the* most important single resource for anyone who wants to grapple with this issue intelligently. One can find the full spectrum of views represented in these works. Theological conservatives who are unacquainted with it (and even some who are writing about abortion give every appearance of such ignorance) may be surprised to find that the most rigorous advocacy of a conservative position on abortion (i.e., the case for a full right to life from the moment of conception) is being produced by secular philosophers who make no appeal to theological assumptions in the course of their argumentation. Of course it is also true that other philosophers have raised serious objections to the conservative position and argued cogently for a radical alternative (viz., that one needs no reasons to morally justify an abortion). The literature on abortion produced by moral philosophers, then, is sophisticated and wide-ranging in its conclusions, and it ought to be required reading for anyone who wants to come to terms with the abortion controversy. This book interacts with that literature and takes it seriously.

But a further element is required before we can begin to speak of a blend, and this element is an interaction with the theological tradition of which I am a part—namely, the Christian tradition, and more specifically, the evangelical wing of Protestantism. I have grounded my reflections in a theological tradition that is orthodox and biblically based while trying not to slight the contributions of the broader Christian community, Protestant and Roman Catholic alike. But having said that, it should not be automatically supposed that I must therefore be committed to a position absolutely antithetical to abortion, that how I reach my conclusions may be of interest (indeed, that should always be of interest) but that the conclusions themselves are fixed before serious argument even begins. That is not the case. In fact, it is part of my purpose to argue that biblical and theological considerations do not *narrowly* limit the positions open to us.

Although I do focus on the theological concerns that many people (including myself) have when confronting the abortion issue, I have also tried to direct the central arguments of this book to the secular community. Because these arguments can undergo a secular as well as a theological translation, they can speak to both religious and secular communities at the same time. I have tried to make my formulations do this double duty.

I have also tried to consider the broadest possible range of arguments, both popular and technical. It is my contention that popular arguments and positions are by no means always lacking in insight, even in the case of those arguments that have no technical counterpart. There is a risk involved in evaluating popular arguments, especially those that lack a more technical or academic version: approaching these arguments and positions in a critical spirit and sensing an easy prey, one might be tempted to give them something less than a fair hearing, overlooking potentially vigorous defenses that they could receive in the hands of competent advocates. I hope I have not done this, but I can offer no guarantee. More than once I have been surprised by competent apologies for positions that I had initially thought weak and unattractive.

It is my purpose here to give all of the principal arguments as fair a hearing as possible, although I do have my own opinion on the issue. I am not crusading for my point of view. Although I judge it to be a reasonable position, I am not so bold as to suggest that it wins out over the other positions hands down. To the contrary, the considerable complexity of the abortion issue suggests to me that some measure of uncertainty is appropriate in whatever position one adopts. Surely I do not suppose that the arguments presented in this book will suffice to eliminate the agony I believe to be rightly involved in most decisions about abortion.

This book originally grew out of a course that I taught at Westmont College entitled "The Morality of Killing." It was a far-ranging exploration of most of the moral issues involving killing that confront contemporary society—abortion, euthanasia, suicide, capital punishment, war, political assassination, terrorism, and the killing of animals. Of all those topics, the one that from the outset struck me as the most morally provocative and intellectually intriguing was the abortion issue. Time has not changed this conviction. This book reflects my attempt at thinking this issue through—a task none of us ought ever to suppose we have completed once and for all.

I wish to thank the editors of *Christian Scholar's Review* for permission to reprint portions of my article "The Right to Life— Reflections on Three Theories" (*CSR,* 13 [1984]: 315-32). I wish also to acknowledge the considerable editorial assistance I received from a former colleague Dwight Small; his kindness and time were more than I had any right to expect. Thanks also to those hardworking typists Betty Bouslough, Lois Gundry, Dottie Brainerd, and Florence Young. Then, of course, to my wife, Eleanore, and my daughter, Siri, whose love and emotional support make this and everything else possible, I give all my gratitude.

1

Procedural Comments

In discussing moral theories on abortion we will use a number of evaluative techniques in an effort to determine which of them we might accept. We need some basis on which to make our choice. Some arguments hold that we ought to repudiate any theory that commits us to approving actions that are immoral. Other arguments hold that we ought to avoid any practice that is likely to produce unwanted social consequences. Some arguments invoke biblical themes to shed light on a particular area of controversy. Other arguments invoke moral principles that are both part of the common moral stock and rooted in the Judeo-Christian tradition. None of these techniques is free of controversy, and so I would like to make some comment about each of them at the outset.

MORAL THEORIES AND THEIR IMPLICATIONS

One important way to test a moral theory is to trace out its implications. If we judge that the implications of a theory are morally unacceptable, then we must judge that the theory itself is unacceptable. For example, if I find that one of the implications of a given moral theory of abortion is that *unfertilized* ova have the right to life, then I might justifiably conclude that the theory requires radical revision. This point has been engagingly made in a more general way by William Gass:

Imagine I approach a stranger on the street and say to him, "If you please, sir, I desire to perform an experiment with your aid." The stranger is obliging, and I lead him away. In a dark place conveniently by, I strike his head with the broad of an axe and cart him home. I place him, buttered and trussed, in an electric oven. The thermostat reads 450° F. Thereupon I go off to play poker with friends and forget all about the obliging stranger in the stove. When I return, I realize I have overbaked my specimen, and the experiment, alas, is ruined.

Something has been done wrong. Or something wrong has been done.

Any ethic that does not roundly condemn my action is vicious. It is interesting that none is vicious for this reason. It is also interesting that no more convincing refutation of any ethic could be given than by showing it approved of my baking the obliging stranger.[1]

Looking at the implications of a particular moral theory for specific cases is simply a way of determining what we are buying when we buy the theory to begin with. This testing procedure is especially important when we move into new areas of moral concern and when we are constructing new and original theories to cover them, for a theory that on the surface seems innocuous enough may surprisingly turn out to have outrageous implications.

Some moral theorists are suspicious of testing procedures that stress our moral response to particular cases. They prefer to deal solely at the level of general principle, arguing that principles or theories ought *always* to be the standard by which we test our moral reactions and never the reverse. Still there is much to be said about confronting a situation in all its particularity with its harms and hurts, its joys and happiness, and then to ask, "Can I accept that? My theory commits me to it, but can I really accept that?" When all is said and done, if I cannot accept the implications of a theory—because, say, it invests an unfertilized ovum with the right to life or it denies that killing infants is wrong in and of itself—then how can I in good conscience accept the theory?

Of course debate will often center on just what the implications of a given theory actually are, its proponents often *denying*

---

1. Gass, "The Case of the Obliging Stranger," in *Philosophic Problems,* ed. Maurice Mandelbaum et al., 2d ed. (New York: Macmillan, 1967), p. 525.

that it has the implications its critics allege. Here honesty and logical rigor are called for—virtues not easily embodied. Logical rigor is always difficult to achieve, and honesty often escapes us when our own theories are at stake. But even when there *is* agreement as to what the implications of a theory are, there may be genuine disagreement about whether they are morally acceptable or not. For example, a growing number of moral philosophers agree that arguments which show that *fetuses* lack a right to life also show that *infants* lack a right to life. Some philosophers are able to accept that implication, while others are horrified by it. In light of this, we might do well to frame our procedural observation in personal terms: If *I* am morally compelled to reject an implication of a theory, then I am also compelled to reject the theory that entails it. Such a position at least allows me to be true to my own moral beliefs, and it also preserves respect for a fundamental demand of reason—namely, consistency.[2] Those operating within the biblical tradition will want to see if they can fit the implications of a theory into the theological framework generated by that tradition. That entails moving beyond the question of how a given implication strikes me personally to the question of how a given implication coheres with the basic insights of the biblical tradition. But more about that later.

When a moral theory is alleged to have embarrassing moral implications, there are only a few moves open to its defenders: (1) they can demonstrate that the theory does not in fact have those implications; (2) they can argue that the implications are not really morally embarrassing; or (3) they can admit the implications and the embarrassment but contend that the evidence on behalf of the theory is so strong that it is easier to learn to live with the embarrassment than to reject the theory. In some cases we may not know whether it is better to give up our theory or our judgment about its implications. All we can do in such circumstances is continue to reflect and await further light as we find ourselves in what we hope will be only a temporary dilemma.

---

2. The contention that consistency in moral matters is a virtue is seldom challenged and hence seldom defended at length; I shall not try to do so here. But for one of those rare challenges, see Richard Taylor, *Good and Evil* (New York: Macmillan, 1970), pp. 175–76.

We should also note, however, that there are two moves *not* legitimately open to a proponent of a theory under this kind of attack. First, it is not sufficient to argue by way of defense that the proponents of the theory would not themselves act on the unacceptable implications. It is, for instance, sometimes argued that despite the fact that a liberal theory of abortion logically leads to a liberal theory of infanticide, people who accept a liberal view of abortion will not act as liberals on infanticide. This will not do. It is the morality of the theory, not the virtue of its proponents or their logical consistency, that is at issue here. It may be true that people are often better than their theories and that they are not inclined to live out the worst implications of those theories; in many cases they may not even grasp the implications of a theory they hold. But that doesn't save the *theory.* On the other hand, if advocates of a morally acceptable theory *erroneously* draw morally objectionable conclusions that they are willing to act on, then that reflects on the advocates of the theory but not on the theory itself. So at issue is what the theory actually commits us to in principle, and in order to determine this we need not know what fallible and sinful advocates of the theory will end up doing.

Second, in order to save a theory from attack it will not do to argue that the morally embarrassing implications are merely theoretical and not applicable to real life. Thus if I have a moral theory that renders obligatory the torture of all Martians, I will not successfully defend my theory by observing that there are no Martians and thus—fortunately—there is no one for me to torture. Not at all. My theory still stands condemned *in principle.* After all, in morals we ought to have commitments that are morally acceptable in principle as well as in fact.

Thus we see that one important test of any moral theory is its congruence with our deeply held moral convictions about particular cases, be they theoretical or real-life cases. To the extent that a given theory is consistent with one's convictions it will find support, and to the extent that it is in conflict with those convictions it will be judged unacceptable. But let's go further. Surely our theories, if they are to be more than mere summaries of what we already believe, must also serve as standards by which we can judge those convictions that make up our common moral consciousness. Thus it should not arouse undue concern if a moral theory we otherwise found acceptable were to come into conflict with moral beliefs that we hold *tenta-*

tively. Such a conflict would not indicate a failure on the part of the theory to account for certain fundamental data required of a normative ethical theory (viz., our *firmly held* moral convictions about particular cases). Further, it seems reasonable to suppose that if a moral theory is supported by our deeply felt moral convictions and at the same time is consistent with recognized moral principles, it in turn can legitimately be used to shed light on those difficult borderline cases in which we are morally unsure of ourselves; indeed, there seems to be no reason why such a theory should not assume authority sufficient to overturn convictions that conflict with the theory, should those convictions be less than firmly held. So if we are to successfully refute a moral theory by drawing out unacceptable implications, we must provide examples of acts that are both obligatory on the basis of that theory and that we strongly feel to be immoral. To the degree, then, that we are in doubt, torn in different directions or perplexed about the moral status of a theory's implications, we must admit that we are not in possession of a decisive refutation.

A WORD ABOUT BAD CONSEQUENCES

There are moral theorists who maintain that only consequences are relevant to the moral evaluation of a practice, their concern usually being with the consquences for human happiness and well-being. While I do not share the conviction that *only* consequences are relevant to the moral evaluation of a practice, I think it cannot be denied that consequences of this kind are of considerable importance in any moral evaluation, and particularly important in assessing any proposal to legalize practices such as abortion. If we can show that the acceptance of a practice will have undesirable consequences, then we will have provided a reason for rejecting the practice. This type of argument is often used in the abortion debate. Some have argued, for example, that abortion will lead to infanticide, infanticide will lead to euthanasia, and euthanasia will ultimately lead to the mass genocide of some racial or religious group. This kind of argument is often referred to in the literature—somewhat derisively—as the "slippery slope" argument: one foot on the slope and over you go, right down to the bottom.

These arguments from consequences vary in their integrity, some being no more than wild and irresponsible charges, while others have a more judicious and credible character. But I wish to suggest that the extent to which we are inclined to believe such arguments is often directly tied to how intrinsically objectionable we judge abortion to be in the first place. If we give abortion a clean bill of moral health, we are far less inclined to have fears over such ugly prospects. It is important for us to recognize this. Often we are confident that the consequences of a practice will be bad on the basis of nothing more than our conviction that the practice is morally objectionable per se. This is the case in many areas of moral concern. For example, many people who think that capital punishment is a morally just act when exacted on the appropriately guilty offender are also inclined to believe that it will set a good example for the community and ultimately deter acts of murder more effectively than lengthy prison terms. Such persons tend to persist in believing this even when the empirical evidence seems contrary to their belief. On the other hand, people who find capital punishment cruel and inhumane are not only strongly inclined to believe that it fails to deter more effectively than lengthy prison terms but are inclined to believe quite the reverse—namely, that it sets a bad example, contributes to a disrespect for human life, and ultimately serves to encourage murderous behavior.

Another interesting example of this phenomenon is found in the words of Pope Paul IV in his 1968 encyclical condemning artificial birth control: "It is also to be feared that the man, growing used to the employment of anti-conceptive practices, may finally lose respect for the woman and, no longer caring for her physical and psychological equilibrium, may come to the point of considering her as a mere instrument of selfish enjoyment and no longer his respected and beloved companion." Thus we are told that the use of artificial birth control is going to lead to the abuse of women by men. After reading and reflecting on these words it is hard not to believe that in this passage Pope Paul is giving in to the universal inclination to expect dire consequences to follow from the widespread acceptance of a practice one presumes to be evil. He believes that using contraceptives is itself morally evil and he assumes that evil will breed evil. Many of us consider the Pope's prediction farfetched, on the other hand, because we consider the use of artificial contraceptive devices to be morally unobjectionable and because we are strongly inclined to believe that morally neutral acts (and acts that serve human interests) are not likely to have bad consequences.

To a considerable extent, then, our view of the world and the causal connections that we believe obtain in it is determined by our moral perspective. This is a key point, because if our confidence that abortion will have a range of bad consequences is determined solely by our prior belief that abortion is intrinsically wrong, then we should recognize that our case against abortion is no stronger than our ability to show that abortion is intrinsically objectionable to begin with, and our appeal to bad consequences will have to be very much a secondary consideration. This is not to say that there are no independent arguments to show the likelihood of certain bad consequences ensuing, but it is to say that such arguments are relatively rare, and that in any case we will tend to warm to them only to the degree that we are already convinced that the activity is itself a bad one.

The bad consequences that a practice may have can take different forms. First, there can be undesirable side effects. In the case of abortion, for example, it might be alleged that it presents too high a risk of maternal death, abortion-induced sterility, or various complications for future pregnancies. Since we have increasingly reliable information on the health risks associated with abortion, however, we are now able (or very nearly able) to judge the validity of such allegations by appeal to the medical data. Still I think that anti-abortion forces have been harder to convince of the safety of abortion than their pro-abortion counterparts; perhaps this indicates some wishful thinking on both sides.

A second kind of bad consequence is that the practice itself may become increasingly widespread. If one judges the practice to be a bad one, then "more of the same" will indeed be a bad consequence. It is to be expected that those who judge the practice to be objectionable will be more sensitive to this possibility and more fearful of any such eventuality.

A third kind of bad consequence is that yet other objectionable practices may follow in the wake of the first. Abortion may lead to infanticide, for instance, and then to euthanasia and genocide. Such consequences are not merely undesirable side effects or simply more of the same thing; rather, they are additional objectionable practices that the critic sees proceeding from the same rationale used to justify the original practice. It is at this point that one's moral perspective tends to determine one's view of the world and the causal connections that obtain in it. We should be especially aware of what is going on whenever we anticipate that bad consequences will flow from some proposed practice even though we lack empirical evidence and can offer no other supporting considerations in favor of such anticipation.

MORAL AUTHORITY

In contemporary intellectual circles, religious as well as secular, appeal to authority is suspect. Indeed, the suggestion that we can determine the rightness or wrongness of abortion or even gain some valuable help by consulting the proper authority is not warmly received. Such an appeal is viewed as turning one's back on an intelligent and thoughtful approach to moral issues and replacing it with a blind trust in one of a myriad of authorities that are competing for our unthinking allegiance. Of course, when the matter is put in those terms it is hard not to agree. But we may wonder whether that is the only way to put the matter.

The philosopher Tom Regan has raised two objections to the use of moral authority. First, he tells us that an appeal to what the Bible teaches won't work because people can't agree on what the Bible teaches:

> The difficulties that exist when Jews and Christians consult the Bible ("God's revelation to Man") can be taken as illustrative. Problems of interpretation abound. Some who think that drinking is wrong think they find evidence in the Bible that God thinks so too; others think they find evidence that He does not. Some who think that homosexuality is declared wrong by God cite what they think are supporting chapters and verses; others cite chapters and verses that they think show God does not think homosexuality is wrong, or they cite the same passages and argue that they should be interpreted differently. The gravity of these and kindred problems of interpretations should not be underestimated.[3]

But if, as Regan says, we should not underestimate this criticism, neither should we overestimate it, for if the appeal to scriptural authority is suspect because there is disagreement over interpre-

---

3. Regan, Introd. in *Matters of Life and Death*, ed. Tom Regan (New York: Random House, 1980), p. 10.

tation of the Bible, then the appeal to reason should be suspect on similar grounds. Moral philosophers attach great importance to the application of reason to moral issues—reason unadulterated by appeals to authority—and yet they also find themselves in radical disagreement over issues such as abortion, disagreeing as much as (if not more than) people who appeal to biblical authority. So if Regan is bewildered by the range of existing interpretations of the Bible (and I hope he has in mind interpretations offered by competent biblical scholars), then perhaps he should be sympathetic to the "Bible believer" who is equally bewildered by the flood of conflicting opinions that flow from the philosophical community on any number of moral issues.

I suspect that Regan's confidence in moral philosophy is really a product of his own thinking about moral issues: he is confident about the results of his own reasoning and consequently is not greatly disturbed by the fact that others disagree with him. But so it is with thoughtful interpreters of Scripture; they too have confidence in their own interpretations and are not greatly disturbed that some people may disagree with them. Indeed, to be scandalized by the fact that biblical interpreters disagree, as Regan is, is the mark of an outsider looking in, of a person who has not seriously brought his or her own interpretative abilities to bear on the biblical text. And of course the same sort of observation applies equally to individuals who despair of moral philosophy because of the seemingly unending disagreements among its practitioners. Being outsiders they don't know which practitioner to believe ("the arguments are complicated and I find them *so* hard to follow"), and consequently they demand complete agreement if they are to take the deliverances of moral philosophy seriously. When this agreement is not forthcoming they simply do what Regan has done with the appeal to scriptural authority—reject it out of hand.

To those who are confounded by the many points of view expressed by moral philosophers we might do well to say, "Think for yourself! Read what capable moral philosophers have written. Do your own moral philosophy. Make up your own mind on these questions." By the same token, we might also do well to tell those who are skeptical about scholarly disagreements in interpretations of the Bible to "interpret Scripture yourself. Become acquainted with competent biblical commentaries. Then do your own interpreting. Make up your own mind on these issues." In the final analysis, the value of any given interpretation of a Scripture passage (on drinking, homosexuality, or whatever) will have to be determined by careful study; nothing is settled by broad statements to the effect that interpreters of Scripture are often at odds with each other, and that therefore there are no interpretations of Scripture of which one can be reasonably confident.

Regan's second objection to moral authority is more substantial, though it does betray a general tendency to see authority as antithetical to reason. In essence, his argument is that in order to identify a revelation as coming from God we must be able to determine on our own (independent of revelation or any other authority) that the content of the supposed revelation is morally acceptable and thus consistent with the character of a good God. Regan makes the point in a general way when he says that

> Even if there is a moral authority, those who are not moral authorities can have no reason for thinking that there is one unless the judgments of this supposed authority can be checked for their truth or reasonableness, and it is not possible to check for this unless what is true or reasonable can be known independently of any reliance on what the supposed authority says. If, however, there must be some independent way of knowing what moral judgments are true or reasonable, the introduction of moral authority will not succeed in providing a method of answering moral questions.[4]

The principle behind Regan's argument appears to be this: if there are good reasons for trusting someone as an authority, then one doesn't need the authority at all. One may properly wonder if Regan's argument does not undercut all appeal to authority. This would be an awkward implication since most of what we claim to know, we in fact know because we (presumably) have justified confidence in certain authorities. Is it not true that we have personally confirmed very little of what we claim to know? Of course, we would insist that it is *rational* for us to trust certain authorities (scientists, historians, etc.), but the reasons we have for trusting them would rarely justify dispensing with them as authorities and substituting ourselves in their place. So in principle there is no reason why we cannot also maintain that we can rationally trust a religious authority (in this

---

4. Regan, p. 10.

case Scripture). That there may be grounds to render this trust rational does not entail that the authority itself be displaced; if it did, trusting an authority could *never* be rational. But obviously we can rationally trust a broad range of authorities.

In part, of course, the very grounds for accepting Scripture as revelatory are moral grounds: Christians find themselves captivated by the moral thrust of Scripture. They have, for example, come to be convinced of their own moral failings through an exposure to the norms of Scripture and consequently have come to see themselves as standing in need of God's grace and forgiveness. This assumes a shared moral vision: Christian men and women concur that the biblical norms ought to be obeyed and its ideals honored, all the while acknowledging that they have failed to do so. Further, the God Christians believe to be addressing them in Scripture is One they judge a fitting object of adoration, thanksgiving, love, and commitment. Is not this response in large measure a moral response? Indeed, worship itself is an act of moral evaluation, being the heartfelt declaration that "God is great and greatly to be praised." So it is not that Scripture hangs heavy over the heads of believers as an oppressive authority, commanding them to do things they find in sharp conflict with their own moral beliefs. Rather, part of what it is to be a Christian believer is to experience a highly significant congruence between one's own moral convictions and the biblical picture of God's character and his moral expectations for humanity. To the extent that this is the case one has a legitimate basis for counting as trustworthy those biblical teachings that presently elude one's own grasp and understanding. That is, because one is personally convinced at so many points that the moral teachings of Scripture are true one is therefore justified in trusting Scripture at those points where its teachings are not so solidly confirmed by one's own personal convictions.

I would make only one qualification in what I have said: one ought never in following an authority to act in a fashion that conflicts with one's persistent and deeply felt moral convictions. Indeed, if a command conflicts with these sorts of convictions, then one has reason to conclude that the command does not originate with God at all but must have some other source. Here Regan is correct: God can command only what is good, and if in fact one is *firmly* convinced that what is commanded is morally bad and one has reasonably excluded all possibility of interpretative error, then one cannot affirm that the command comes from God. One could, of course, conclude that one's persistent and deeply felt moral convictions are mere delusions, but that is not easily done. There is no reason to believe that a good and gracious God—the God and Father of Jesus Christ—would ever demand that persons do what they sincerely and conscientiously believe to be wrong, Kierkegaard's use of the biblical account of Abraham's sacrificial offering of Isaac notwithstanding. For Abraham, in that famous Old Testament account (see Genesis 22), did not set aside his conviction that human sacrifice was wrong so that he might be obedient to the command of God (Kierkegaard's "teleological suspension of the ethical"). Abraham did not perceive any conflict or tension between a general duty not to make human sacrifice on the one hand and obedience to God's particular command to sacrifice Isaac on the other. In Abraham's case, human sacrifice was *not* in itself morally unacceptable; he lived in a time and a culture that did not condemn such practices. In any case, the biblical story is not presented for the purpose of honoring a faith in God so strong that it will do what is morally repugnant in his name. Rather, it is presented to illustrate a faith so strong that the prospect of Isaac's death did not alter Abraham's confidence that God would keep his promise that through Isaac a great nation would descend (Gen. 21:12), an interpretation with which the New Testament concurs (Heb. 11:17-19). One may consider such faith foolish in a purely rational sense, but it is not *morally* foolish.

More in keeping with the biblical perspective than Kierkegaard's understanding are the Apostle Paul's words when he addressed the issue in his day of Christians' eating meat offered to idols (something Paul himself did not consider inherently objectionable): "But if a person has doubts about what he eats, God condemns him when he eats it, because his action is not based on faith. And anything that is not based on faith is sin" (Rom. 14:23). The Apostle holds that whatever cannot be done in good conscience is sin, and one would hardly expect the Apostle's God to demand that people do what they cannot in good conscience do; God, in such circumstances, would be demanding that people sin!

So, with the proviso that commitment to a moral authority never carries with it the obligation to do what in good conscience one cannot do, we can hold a view of authority that need not be frightening to us; in adopting such a view, we are in no way opening the door to the terrible prospect of following in the footsteps of Kierkegaard's Abraham or in the footsteps of the Rev. Jim Jones to Guyana. In fact, biblical moral teachings have much the same relationship to the Christian's moral consciousness as confirmed moral theories have to the moral consciousness of their advocates. For the most part believers confidently hold the teachings of the Bible to be true—not coldly and mechanically true, like listings in a telephone directory, but personally true; they embrace the teachings as their own strongly held moral beliefs. And naturally, where the teaching of Scripture conflicts with their less firmly held moral convictions, believers defer to the authority of Scripture, doing exactly what adherents to a moral theory would do in similar circumstances. Understandably, whenever believers are morally perplexed or uncertain, they seek direction from biblical teaching, just as adherents to a moral theory will return to that theory when they encounter a comparable perplexity. But what, it may be asked, is to be done when firmly held and persistent moral convictions are at odds with biblical directives? In that case we would have the making of a decisive counter-example. But this, of course, is what believers in Scripture (and believers in a moral theory) are convinced cannot be produced for that is what it means to be a believer.

BAPTIZING MORAL CONCLUSIONS

When Christians reason about moral matters, they often follow a procedure indistinguishable from that followed by a thoughtful secularist. They appeal to widely recognized principles (principles that are by no means the exclusive possession of Christians), they test moral theories by drawing out their implications, and they point to the possible bad consequences of adopting a particular practice. Sometimes this similarity in procedure is not evident, even to Christians themselves, because of the spiritual terminology that often accompanies Christian dialogue, but the fact remains that it is not *how* Christians go about reaching moral conclusions that distinguishes them from secularists so much as what they do with those conclusions once they are reached: the Christian accepts them as the will of God and construes acting on them as acting in obedience to God. As Keith Ward has put it, Christians are "disposed to conceive of the moral life as obedience to a Divine intention";[5] they perceive

---

5. Ward, *Ethics and Christianity* (London: Allen & Unwin, 1970).

an act of honoring a moral conclusion as a way of being obedient to God. This is to say that the Christian's pattern of moral reasoning is not always X *is the will of God* (determined by appropriate biblical exegesis), *therefore I ought to do X.* Often it is just the reverse. The Christian reasons X *is what I ought to do* (determined by methods of moral reflection held in common with the secularist), *therefore X is the will of God.* That is, the Christian baptizes his conclusions, embracing them as God's will. In fact, the Christian is often forced to do this because moral concern focuses on practices that are not directly addressed in Scripture, and biblical themes may only have an oblique application to the issue at hand. In such instances, one cannot get quick chapter-and-verse solutions, but must engage in much the same moral reasoning that any thoughtful person would engage in. To be sure, appeal is made to biblical moral principles, but those principles are often (though not always) a common moral stock that might be used by the secularist as well.

Baptizing a moral conclusion entails more than simply affirming that the moral conclusion supplied by reason is the will of God, however; the task also involves finding a biblical home for those conclusions. This means relating the moral conclusions that one has reached to theological themes. As an illustration, consider the recent concern with the construction of an ecological ethic. There is now a growing conviction that we human beings have an obligation to the natural order that transcends the mere use of that order for our own ends. Thus, concern with endangered species is not merely a concern for human welfare. It is not that we wish to save endangered species merely so that they will remain available as sources of food or clothing or whatever. Our concern goes beyond that. We judge it undesirable and perhaps even tragic that a whole species with its unique genetic treasure should vanish from the face of the earth.

However, there is a way to link this concern for endangered species (and other ecological concerns as well) to biblical themes. The principal theme is that of dominion. In the biblical message, God charges humankind to "have dominion over the fish of the sea and over the birds of the air and over every living thing that moves upon the earth" (Gen. 1:29). Can not this charge reasonably be understood to mean that humanity has been assigned the role of stewards of creation, that we are not simply to be users of the created order but preservers and protectors also? We are like caretakers of an estate that can be used temporarily but must ultimately be returned intact and in good working order to its owner. Would this not include a concern for endangered species that lack any utilitarian value—they being part of that estate? It would seem so. But notice that somewhere along the line we have to make some sort of determination about the value of particular species. Thus, how much effort, energy, and human resources should we expend to save this or that species? No doubt we should save the whale from extinction. But at what cost? And should the snail darter be the object of the same concern as the whale? Or the coyote? We have to answer these questions (and a host of others) before we can fully know how we are to conduct ourselves as faithful stewards of the created order. Being told that we are to be faithful stewards does not by itself provide us with any answers. But once we have secured our answers by normal methods of reasoning, we will be in a position to carry out our role as faithful stewards, and thus in a position to baptize our moral conclusions into our faith. And why does the Christian engage in this kind of baptizing activity, relating moral conclusions to theological themes? The answer is found in the words of Keith Ward that I just quoted: the Christian is "disposed to conceive of the moral life as obedience to a Divine intention." Thus, this act of what I have called baptism serves the purpose of connecting one's moral perceptions to the divine intention by means of recognized theological themes.

THEOLOGICAL THEMES AS MORAL ILLUMINATORS

Theological themes are more than material by means of which the Christian can construe moral conclusions as the will of God. They are also illuminators that can sensitize us to values that we might otherwise fail to notice, and they can give direction to our moral focus. The theological theme of dominion, for example, may not tell us how much human energy ought to be directed to saving the whale, but it does legitimize this as an area of moral concern; ecology, therefore, is a matter appropriate for Christian reflection and action.

There are other theological themes that set other moral agenda for us. The Judeo-Christian tradition affirms that God is the author of all life, and that human life in particular is a gift to be cherished and valued. Indeed, as James Gustafson comments, "If we have received life and its benefits from God's goodness, in a living gratitude what is available to us is not ours to serve only our own interests, to mutilate, to exhaust, to destroy wantonly, to deprive others of."[6] Because abortion terminates human life, it has to be an object of moral concern for the Christian community. To say this is not, of course, to answer a host of questions that we may have: Does a newly fertilized ova have a right to life? Is a later abortion morally more serious than an earlier one? Can a right to life be a matter of degree? Under what circumstances—if any—can an abortion be justified? Nevertheless, the theological theme of life as a gift and a trust from God does certify the legitimacy of these questions and at least tells us that abortion cannot be a matter of moral indifference. At the outset, then, the Christian community must part company with those who say that abortion poses no moral problem, that it is merely a question of what is in the best interests of the pregnant woman and of society. As it stands, then, the relevant theological theme by itself does not *solve* our moral problems so much as it *raises* them, establishing a moral agenda for us and defining the area within which we might seek the answers. We ought not to look to Scripture as a kind of moral thesaurus containing the answers to all our ethical questions when often it is to serve instead as a storehouse of theological themes that give us a perspective from which we can ourselves tackle the problems at hand and work out our answers.

A WORD ABOUT TERMINOLOGY AND EMOTIONS

Having made some preliminary procedural comments, I would also like to make some comments about terminology. In part because the debate over abortion has been so public, partisan, and emotional, it has been characterized by much prejudicial rhetoric. The use of such language is more appropriate to propaganda than to reasoned debate.

There are two principal types of excess that need to be avoided. First, there is the use of highly inflammatory language that is chosen primarily because of its emotive content. Speaking of mothers who would "slaughter their innocent children in the womb" is a case in point. Such language judges the issue prior to any consideration of relevant arguments. Perhaps one would

---

6. Gustafson, *Can Ethics Be Christian?* (Chicago: University of Chicago Press, 1975), p. 102.

be justified in using this kind of strong language after having analyzed the arguments and come to a reasoned conclusion, but to insist from the outset that this is how matters are to be described is not helpful. In any case, it should be a practical consideration that the use of inflammatory language will eventually wear thin. At worst it will provoke an antagonistic response; at best it will be ignored: one who is too shrill for too long will simply not be heard after a while. But there is a second excess that is equally serious—the use of language that hides from us the realities of what we are doing. A classic example is the definition of abortion as "the removal of the products of conception." Such a bland, antiseptic use of language obscures the nature of the action and is every bit as objectionable as its inflammatory counterpart. There are many other ways to slant matters in order to obscure the full character of our actions as well. Consider, for instance, the following advice: "If you don't want to bring an unwanted child into the world, have an abortion." The presumption here is that what is in the womb is not yet in the world, that abortion simply prevents individuals from entering the world—and that before individuals are in the world our responsibility for them is minimal, however considerable it may be after they are in the world. But we may very well wonder whether being in the womb is not being in the world, since the womb is, after all, in the world. Clearly it is not fair simply to sidestep this issue rhetorically rather than dealing with it openly.

This much said, I would like at the outset to note some of the key terms I will be using and also make clear what meanings I will be attaching to them. When I speak of a *zygote* I will be referring to the fertilized ovum as a single-cell entity. In speaking of an *embryo* I will be referring to a developing human organism during the first eight weeks following conception. Technically speaking, the term *fetus* refers to the developing human organism during the period from eight weeks after conception to birth, although in more common usage it can also refer to the developing human organism at *any* stage of development between conception and birth. I will frequently be using the term *fetus* in this broad and nontechnical sense. On those occasions when I need to use the term in its technical sense, I will be using it in conjunction with the other technical terms, *zygote* and *embryo*. So unless the context indicates otherwise, *fetus* should be understood to be referring to the unborn at any stage of development between conception and birth. I realize that some may object to the use of the term *fetus* to describe the unborn on the grounds that it seems too cold and technical, that it has its origins in animal husbandry. To kill what is called a *fetus* may not seem so objectionable as killing what is called a *baby*. But I consider the term *baby* to be prejudicial and inappropriate in the context of the abortion debate: prejudicial because it conjures up the image of a cuddly infant in its bassinet, surrounded by the paraphernalia of the nursery, and inappropriate because a newly fertilized ovum simply is not yet a baby however strong its claim to a right to life may be. The term *unborn* may be more satisfactory to those who object to *fetus*. Indeed, I think it a fair enough term and consequently I shall use it from time to time, even though I realize that some consider it to be shorthand for "unborn baby" and thus, again, prejudicial and inappropriate; I will be using it on the presumption that it does not bear those prejudicial connotations. I hope that by using both *unborn* and *fetus* I can avoid giving any implicit advantage to any of the parties to the abortion debate.

2

Posing the Problem

Fifteen years ago Daniel Callahan stated that "Abortion is a nasty problem, a source of social and legal discord, moral uncertainty, medical and psychiatric confusion, and personal anguish."[1] That is as true today as it was when Callahan first said it, and it is easy to predict that it will be just as true in another fifteen years. Of course, in one sense this is not the case for the individual who holds that no woman is ever justified in aborting a pregnancy on the grounds that abortion is a straightforward case of murder; nor is it the case for the person who views ending the life of a fetus as of no more moral consequence than cosmetic surgery. Neither of these sorts of individuals finds a genuine moral problem here. Perhaps they hold that there is a cause to be served, legislators and judges to be influenced, and a public to be educated, but they do not find any occasion for moral perplexity, and hence they feel no need to work at resolving it.

It seems, however, that for conscientious, thoughtful persons at least some measure of moral uncertainty is appropriate. It has to be admitted that we have not yet resolved all abortion-related issues (theological, philosophical, and moral) satisfactorily, have not yet carefully drawn all the important implications

---

1. Callahan, *Law, Choice and Morality* (New York: The Macmillan Company, 1970), p. 1.

of the various positions on abortion, have not yet dispelled all the conceptual confusion surrounding this issue. Indeed, the issue of abortion continues to be heatedly debated in the courts, in state legislatures, in prestigious academic journals, on television talk shows, in the editorial page letters columns of local newspapers, and so on. Unfortunately, much (though not all) of this discussion takes the form of highly polemical and emotional efforts at converting others. While there is nothing wrong with seeking to convince others of the validity of one's own moral position—indeed, it is often incumbent upon us to do so—these efforts frequently take a form that substitutes psychological persuasion for rational argumentation. And it must be said that both pro-abortion and anti-abortion forces are guilty of this, at least at the popular level. It is desirable, then, to approach this issue in a spirit of fairness that avoids polemical extremes. No doubt when all is said there will still be moral uncertainties and loose ends, but this is not incompatible with some progress and new insight.

Three principal factors have combined to make abortion the serious moral and social problem it is today: (1) abortion is a relatively low risk, pain-free operation when performed by skilled medical practitioners, (2) there are impressive reasons prompting women to seek abortions, and (3) abortion involves terminating the life of what is (minimally) a potential person endowed with some measure of value that warrants respect. We should take a closer look at each of these factors.

THE RISKS

First, the risks to the life and physical health of the woman undergoing medical abortion are *relatively* few as a result of modern medical techniques and competent physicians. However, this has not always been so. Prescriptions for abortion go back some 5,000 years, which indicates that the desire of some women to terminate pregnancies and methods to induce abortion have both been with us for millennia.[2] It boggles the imagination to realize that such ancient prescriptions included the suggestion that the pregnant woman belly flop into the sea from a high cliff. As a suggestion this is perhaps humorous, but as a

---

2. For an examination of the history of abortion, see Lawrence Lader, *Abortion* (New York: Bobbs-Merrill, 1966).

suggestion acted upon it is tragic. Sadly, the history of induced abortion is the history of such tragedies, a history which includes not only the woman who mounts the cliff and dives into the sea but also the more contemporary instance of the woman who visits an illegal backstreet abortionist, receives an injection of a detergent solution, is admitted to a hospital several days afterward suffering from "soap intoxication," and dies within ten days.

Prior to 1850 all methods of terminating a pregnancy posed a serious threat to the woman's life. Any surgery, including abortion, brought with it three chances in eight that the patient would die. However, in the case of legal abortions performed in modern accredited hospitals, the statistics are radically different. Left behind are the horrors of a primitive past along with the crudities of the hack abortionist. Here the patient finds herself in the safe hands of the modern medical doctor, who insures that the risk to her life and comfort is comparatively negligible. In point of fact, there is less risk in aborting a pregnancy—certainly in the early months—than in going through with it to childbirth.

The figures from Great Britain listed in Table A help place the risk of death from abortion in perspective.

Table A

MORTALITY RATES FOR SELECTED SURGICAL PROCEDURES*

OPERATION	NUMBER OF DEATHS PER 100,000 OPERATIONS
Legal abortion	
First trimester	1.7
Second trimester	12.2
Tonsillectomy without adenoidectomy	3.0
Tonsillectomy with adenoidectomy	5.0
Ligation and division of fallopian tubes	5.0
Partial mastectomy (simple mastectomy)	74.0
Lower section Caesarean	111.0
Abdominal hysterectomy	204.0
Appendectomy	352.0

* Source: Malcolm Potts et al., *Abortion* (Cambridge: Cambridge University Press, 1979), p. 211.

Also of interest are the figures in Table B, a breakdown of the abortion death rate for the period 1972–80 in the USA.

Table B

MATERNAL MORTALITY RATES FOLLOWING ABORTIONS
AT VARIOUS STAGES OF PREGNANCY*

GESTATIONAL AGE OF FETUS	NUMBER OF DEATHS PER 100,000 OPERATIONS
8 weeks or less	0.5
9–10	1.3
11–12	2.1
13–15	4.8
16–20	12.8
over 21	15.3

*Source: *Abortion Surveillance, 1979–80* (Atlanta: Center for Disease Control, May 1983), p. 43.

One can see how abortion involves an increasing risk to the life of the mother as the pregnancy is allowed to proceed, the big jump in this regard taking place in the 16- to 20-week period. But to place this in proper perspective, it also needs to be pointed out that there are 9.1 maternal deaths per 100,000 *live* births.[3] But with approximately 95 percent of all abortions now taking place before 16 weeks, the risk for most women having an abortion is appreciably less than it would be for them had they had a live birth.

However, risks to the life of the patient are not the only hazards that may accompany medically induced abortions. It has been hypothesized that induced abortions might impair a woman's subsequent capacity for reproduction, although this does not seem to constitute a threat of sufficient magnitude to deflect most women from seeking an abortion. Indeed, secondary infertility and an increased vulnerability to ectopic pregnancy may result from complicated abortions, but such effects are rare. The frequency of mid-trimester spontaneous abortion among women who have had one previous abortion is the same as that for women having their first pregnancy. The same is true regarding statistics for a shortened gestation period, which entails risk to the life and health of the newborn: there is no difference between mothers who have had an induced abortion and mothers who

3. U.S. Department of Commerce, *Statistical Abstract of the United States 1984* (Washington, D.C.: GPO, 1984), p. 77.

have not in the case of firstborn infants.[4] There is some concern that there may be an association between induced abortion and an increased incidence of breast cancer, but this risk has not yet been confirmed.[5] Thus we can see that modern medical practice has removed most of the risk (always a relative notion) from abortion along with the pain. Even the inconvenience has been eliminated: a woman can go to a clinic in the early stages of a pregnancy, have an abortion by vacuum extraction, and leave within hours. The inhibiting factor of risk having been removed along with most legal restrictions, more women are seeking abortions for reasons that many would judge to be less than significant—perhaps even trivial—in the light of the fact that they are ending a developing human life. And because women are seeking abortions for a wide range of reasons, we are confronted with the task (if we choose to engage in moral reflection) of weighing those reasons and asking ourselves under what circumstances—if any—a woman is justified in terminating a pregnancy.

THE REASONS

The second consideration that should prompt us to take the abortion issue seriously is the impressive list of reasons that prompt many women to seek an abortion.

1. The Medical Ground

The most dramatic case, of course, is that of the woman whose life is at risk. There is, for example, ectopic pregnancy. One in every two hundred pregnancies is ectopic, which is to say that it involves an embryo implanted outside the uterus, usually in the fallopian tubes, which are not adequately elastic to accommodate its growth. Unless the pregnancy is terminated, the mother will experience internal hemorrhaging and may die. Or consider the case of a pregnant woman with a serious heart condition who may not be able to survive a live birth, her heart

---

4. These comments are based on a summary of 150 studies from 21 countries; see *Abortion Surveillance, 1979–80* (Atlanta: Center for Disease Control, 1983), pp. 14–15.

5. See Willard Cates, Jr., "Legal Abortion: The Public Health Record," *Science* 215 (March 1982): 1589–90.

being unable to meet the demands placed on it during delivery. Or consider the case of a pregnant woman whose uterus has been diagnosed as cancerous: she may have to have her uterus removed immediately by surgery, killing the embryo-fetus, if she is to have any realistic hope of surviving. None of these examples are common occurrences, but they do happen from time to time.

2. The Psychiatric Ground

The emotional and psychological well-being of the woman may be at stake. In some instances a woman may be suicidal as a result of the pregnancy or risk serious psychiatric illness should she continue with the pregnancy. In such situations it may be tempting to conclude that the only solution is abortion.

3. The Criminal Ground

Pregnancies that result from forcible rape or incest pose an undeniably serious problem for the pregnant woman. It is true that pregnancies resulting from rape are rare (perhaps because women are less likely to conceive under such traumatic circumstances), but the infrequency of such pregnancies does not alter the nature of the moral problem that confronts us. To deny a woman an abortion in such cases is to make her carry through with a pregnancy that was forced on her to begin with. Pregnancies resulting from incestuous relations involve two other problems: first, the pregnancy carries with it a significant social stigma, which may result in subsequent emotional scars for the woman; and second, there is an increased risk that any children produced by sexual relations between individuals who are closely related biologically will suffer physical deformities and mental retardation.

4. The Eugenic Ground

There may be indications that if a given pregnancy is permitted to go to term the baby will be physically abnormal or mentally retarded. A broad range of congenital abnormalities can be reliably diagnosed by amniocentesis (a procedure in which fluid is drawn from the amniotic sack and tested), and the woman may then be confronted by the choice of aborting the pregnancy or giving birth to a deformed or retarded infant.[6]

5. The Socio-economic Ground

In some cases pressing financial circumstances make a pregnancy a very considerable burden. If a pregnancy leads to a loss of work for a woman who provides the sole support for a large family, the financial burden could be critical. When a woman's family is already too large for her to care for it adequately, an additional child could entail real hardship for all family members.

6. The Ground of Extreme Youth

When a pre-teen-ager or a girl in her early teens becomes pregnant, she may simply not have the emotional stability or maturity to carry through with the pregnancy. The burden that she and her family would have to bear would be a heavy one.

7. The Personal Ground

A woman may find pressing personal reasons prompting her to seek an abortion. An unwanted pregnancy might well ruin her chances to realize important life goals and aspirations, for instance. Consider the case of a woman whose children are grown and who is finally about to embark on her own long-delayed career but who once more finds herself pregnant. The sacrifice involved in carrying through with a pregnancy under such circumstances might very well be considerable.

Within most of these seven categories one can formulate any number of specific arguments for abortion, some substantial in nature and others no doubt frivolous. To talk of emotional and psychological well-being, for example, is to introduce everything from a temporary emotional disturbance to a serious and perhaps permanent psychiatric disorder. Personal grounds for abor-

---

6. An added problem in this instance is that amniocentesis cannot be initiated until the fourteenth week of pregnancy, and it takes from two to six weeks to obtain the results (cultures of cells have to be grown in the amniotic fluid that has been extracted). This could mean that the woman would be in the twentieth week of pregnancy by the time she is in a position to make an abortion decision.

tion might range all the way from a desire not to delay a planned trip to Europe to a desire not to have career plans forever frustrated. Economic considerations could vary from a minor financial setback to significant hardship. In the matter of eugenic considerations, we need to note that prospective deformity or retardation can range from slight to considerable, and the probabilities involved can range from high to extremely low. But it is important to note that there are many cases in each area that involve quite impressive reasons for wanting an abortion. This is not to suggest that even these impressive reasons in themselves justify the deliberate termination of a pregnancy and the consequent death of developing fetal life, but it is to suggest that these reasons at least pose a serious problem for us. The issue here is not whether some or many or even most of the million and a half women annually seeking and obtaining abortions in the United States are doing so without substantial reasons. The point is that good reasons or substantial grounds for abortions do exist, and we should feel the force of them even if we eventually conclude that these "good" reasons are simply not good enough to justify the act.

THE FETUS

The third factor involved in making abortion a moral problem for us is the value that attaches to the fetus—and it would seem that everyone ought at least to grant that the fetus does have some special value. To have an abortion out of curiosity (in order to find out what the fetus looks like, say) or to terminate a five-month pregnancy so as not to delay a trip to Europe would strike most people as evidences of an unjustifiable disregard for the value of developing human life. It would be more than objectionable on grounds of mere bad taste; it would be *morally* objectionable. But as soon as we acknowledge that not all reasons are good enough to justify having an abortion, we have acknowledged that the fetus has some value that should be recognized, and we are consequently obliged to deal with the conflicting values and claims that confront us in making an abortion decision.

One cannot but be impressed with the kind of biological data that right to life groups emphasize, regardless of what its moral import may be. It does seem incontestable, for instance, that from the point of conception there exists a living organism (by any standard biology textbook definition of life) that can die and consequently can be killed. Therefore, this much has to be recognized: abortions kill, for where there is no killing there is no abortion. Further, it is *human* biological life that is terminated. For just as I am a human adult, so the zygote is a human zygote, the embryo a human embryo, and the fetus a human fetus: they are not canine or feline. Nor is this human life simply a part of the woman's body like her kidneys or gall bladder. To be sure, it is dependent upon the nurture provided by her body, but it is not an organ of that body. Fetal life has its own genetic makeup, its own blood supply and circulation (the blood of mother and fetus do not intermingle), and its own principle of growth. Developing fetal life is nourished and sustained by means of the placenta, but the growth principle is its own and not the mother's.

Further, fetal development is impressive and awe-inspiring to contemplate. From the point of conception there is a unique genetic package with all the encoded information necessary for the unfolding of a full-fledged human being. From the very outset all inherited characteristics are genetically built into the organism. As early as the third and fourth week the fetus has a heartbeat and a functioning circulatory system. By the sixth week all fetal organs are present in rudimentary form. By the seventh week the fetus responds to stimuli. Brain waves can be recorded by the eighth week (even earlier in some cases). By the ninth week the fetus is swallowing, squinting its eyes, and exhibiting reflexive movement. By the twelfth week the basic structure of the brain is complete.

Unquestionably, one of the most effective ways to inculcate respect for fetal life is simply to provide a description, replete with pictures, of what is taking place in the womb of the pregnant woman. There need be no moralizing or abstract argumentation, but only an objective account of the biological data.[7] Ultimately, of course, we have to go beyond such descriptions and reflect on their import, but they do serve to make it difficult to accept the contention that fetal life has no value at all or that it has value only to the extent that it is wanted by others and that abortion is merely elective surgery, no more and no less. To

---

7. For an example of what I have in mind, see Geraldine Lux Flanagan, *The First Nine Months of Life* (New York: Simon & Schuster, 1965).

be sure, the fetus is not self-conscious, is not yet a rational being, and has no desires, hopes, or aspirations that will be frustrated by death. But neither does the newborn infant possess rationality, have desires, or the like, and yet most people would be reluctant to kill infants with the same regularity with which we now kill fetuses. Both the fetus and the newborn are biological human life on the way to becoming personal human life. To be sure there is a lag time of a few months between them—personal life will emerge in the infant before it does in the fetus—but we may well ponder whether this difference is sufficient to justify our aborting (i.e., killing) fetal life with an easy conscience.

FETAL BRAIN DEVELOPMENT

The most significant feature of fetal growth in terms of the abortion controversy is the fact that the biological basis for personal life is developing. Specifically, this means that the brain and central nervous system are developing, for it is the human brain that makes possible the rational life that we associate with human beings.

Different parts of the brain grow at different speeds. During the first three months following conception, the midbrain and spinal cord are the most advanced in growth, followed by the pons and medulla, the cerebral hemisphere, and lastly the cerebellum. The cerebral hemisphere is that part of the brain believed to be crucially involved in cognitive functions, but it lags behind various other parts during the brain's early development, the developing fetus being primarily dependent upon its lower brain regions. We may be impressed that at eleven weeks the fetus will make swallowing movements if its lips are touched; at fourteen weeks it will grimace and rotate its pelvis in an attempt to avoid the stimulus of having its face touched; at twenty-eight weeks its face will express pleasure when fed sugar and revulsion when fed salt water—but we should note that none of these responses is the result of a cerebral function; similar responses have been obtained from malformed infants whose brains have not developed beyond the pons or brain stem.[8] In fact, the fetus does not employ its cerebral cortex in any significant way as far

8. See Steven Rose, *The Conscious Brain* (New York: Knopf, 1974), p. 156; and W. A. Marshall, *Development of the Brain* (Edinburgh: Oliver & Boyd, 1968), p. 16.

as is known. Its reflex activity is regulated by the lower brain regions, not by the cerebral cortex. And this is also true of the newborn infant. As Stephen Rose has put it, "The one-month-old baby is plainly still a subcortical organism."[9]

That much said, we can still note a number of stages in the course of fetal development that seem significant. At forty days, for instance, electro-encephalographs have recorded brain waves.[10] This indicates brain activity of some kind at a very early stage, although the level of development is still very primitive and certainly insufficient to support the emergence of personal life. In fact, "If our brain stopped growing at this stage [five weeks], we'd rank with the primitive fish on the I.Q. scale."[11]

At eight weeks the fetus has an anatomically formed brain, although the nerve cells are undifferentiated. As Paul Chauchard notes, it is the maturing of the nervous system that more than anything else renders the fetal organism a unity and not simply a collection of cells.[12] At eight weeks the cerebral cortex also begins to acquire its typical cells.[13]

Spontaneous movements (in contrast to mere muscular reactions to external stimuli) occur during the ninth week and are indicative of a maturing medulla (the part of the brain that plays a role in swallowing, speaking, and regulating the heart, blood pressure, and breathing). At five and a half months the respiratory center of the medulla is operational. Cerebral maturation begins between six and seven months.[14]

With birth we simply have a continuation of fetal development. No miraculous transformation of brain activity occurs at this point. It is not until the tenth day after birth that the neocortex (that part of the cerebral cortex peculiar to mammals and man that is responsible for the higher mental functions) shows signs of change, becoming excitable in a weak and diffuse way. Gradually thereafter, automatic movements are brought under cortical control.

---

9. Rose, p. 158.

10. See Hannibal Hamlin, "Life or Death by E.E.G.," *Journal of the American Medical Association* 190 (12 October 1964): 113.

11. John Pfeiffer, *The Human Brain* (New York: Harper & Row, 1955), p. 34.

12. Chauchard, *The Brain* (New York: Grove Press, 1962), pp. 49–50.

13. Leslie Brainerd Arey, *Developmental Anatomy* (Philadelphia: W. B. Saunders, 1965), p. 106b.

14. H. Tuchmann-Duplessis et al., *Illustrated Human Embryology* (New York: Springer-Verlag, 1973), vol. 3, *Nervous System and Endocrine Glands*, p. 82.

By way of summing up, we should note that both the fetus and the newborn are subcortical organisms. This means we cannot differentiate the one from the other on the basis of an active neocortex. Indeed, this center of the higher mental functions does not begin to come into play until the infant's period of primary socialization (five weeks to seven months after birth). During the fetal period, *sub*cortical brain regions are growing and are increasingly active, but this is also the case for anencephalic individuals, who will never develop into persons, lacking as they do the upper brain regions. Though necessary for the subsequent emergence of personal life, the lower brain regions are not physiologically sufficient to bring this about. But normally (tragic brain deformities aside) development of the lower brain regions occurs in an organism that is *also* developing (at a slower rate) those upper brain regions critically involved in higher mental functions.

In light of this information, a couple of key points are worth stressing. First, we cannot seek to downgrade the value of the fetus or minimize the strength of its claim to life on the ground that it is a subcortical being without doing the same for the newborn, which is also subcortical. Second, we ought not to make too much of the fact that the fetus sucks its thumb, eagerly swallows amniotic fluid injected with sugar, and so on, since the anencephalic, which has no chance of developing into a person, will do the same. Indeed, we might well suppose that a chimpanzee fetus evinces similar behavior.

3
Persons, Souls, and Fetuses

In the abortion debate, much controversy has centered on the nature of personhood and whether fetuses are truly persons or merely potential persons. It is often maintained that if fetuses are no more than potential persons then we can proceed to abort them with few qualms, but that if they are persons then abortion is a very serious matter indeed. Hence the importance of asking "Is the fetus a person?" Much of the literature on abortion has been directed at providing an answer to this question, but in the end it may not be quite so crucial as many people have supposed. The fact is that conservatives (i.e., advocates of a right to life from conception) need not argue that the fetus is a person in the strict or paradigmatic sense, and the liberals (i.e., those who take a permissive stance on the abortion question) need not categorically deny that fetuses are persons in order to make their respective cases.

Should we conclude that fetuses are only potential persons, it does not automatically follow that conservatives would have to capitulate to liberals on the abortion issue; they could simply argue that the kind of potential for personhood that the fetus has invests it with a right to life. After all, it might be argued that newborn infants have a right to life, and they have that right solely by virtue of their potential for personhood, so the fetus's potential personhood should be sufficient to give it a strong claim to life too. Conservatives, then, need not become agitated

Not constitutional (handwritten margin note)

over the denial that fetuses are persons unless it is accompanied by the claim that only persons have a right to life. But this the conservative can deny. Of course, this denial would call for extended argument, along with some possible qualifications along the way.[1] But making the conservative case in such an argument would be no more problematic than arguing for the claim that fetuses are persons in order to settle the abortion debate.

On the other hand, should we conclude that fetuses *are* persons, liberals would not have to capitulate to the conservatives. Liberals could grant that the term *person* covers everything from human fetuses to human adults while nonetheless observing that within the class of persons there are two main subclasses: those who have a potential for rationality (e.g., fetuses), and those whose potential for rationality has been actualized (e.g., normal healthy adults). It could then be argued that those in the first subclass have a much weaker claim to life than those in the second subclass—sufficiently weaker to substantiate an argument that abortion would be justified in at least a fair number of the situations in which women are confronted with an unwanted pregnancy. To be sure, much additional argumentation would have to be marshalled in support of such a contention, but the point once more is that the abortion issue would not be settled by a simple determination of whether the fetus is a person.[2]

Surely, with these considerations in mind, we should not expect that an analysis of the concept of *person* is going to yield a quick and decisive outcome to the abortion debate. In fact, there could be some value to banning the use of the term "person" in the context of the abortion dispute and talking

---

1. A conservative might choose not to argue that fetuses and infants have a right to life, for example, but simply that killing what has a natural potential for personal life is intrinsically wrong.

2. After arguing the plausibility of the thesis that persons come into existence at conception, Roderick Chisholm comments (without further elaboration), "Surely it is right, sometimes to terminate a pregnancy.... Doubtless such acts always call for an excuse. But let us not pretend that, when we perform them, probably we are not causing anyone to cease to be. Let us have the courage to face the moral facts of the matter: Occasionally it *is* right for one person to annihilate another" ("Coming into Being and Passing Away: Can the Metaphysician Help?" in *Language, Metaphysics and Death*, ed. John Donnelly [New York: Fordham University Press, 1978], p. 23).

instead of (1) those who have a *potential* capacity for rationality and (2) those who have a *developed* capacity for rationality. Then we might simply ask: Do both have a right to life? Do both have an *equally* strong claim to life? For indeed a great deal of the abortion debate finally comes down to just these two questions. Nevertheless, for good or ill the term *person* is very much a part of most traditional arguments concerning abortion, and so in what follows I shall continue to use it even though my particular use of the term will not settle the debate.

THE PERSON: A STRICT CONSTRUCTION

A person is in a strict sense a being who possesses the developed capacity to engage in acts of *intellect* (to think, to use language, etc.), acts of *emotion* (to love, to hate, etc.), and acts of *will* (to make moral choices, to affirm spiritual ideals, etc.).[3] Most certainly it is the case that human beings are more valuable than dogs, cats, and horses precisely because they can engage in just these sorts of acts, whereas dogs, cats, and horses cannot—or at least cannot do them to the degree that typical human beings can.[4] It is because we have this threefold capacity that we are

---

3. An individual who could think and will but never experienced any emotions (a Mr. Spock of *Star Trek* fame, for example) would no doubt be a person, though quite different from any person we have ever known. But since persons as we know them are in fact emotional beings, I have included this dimension in my definition.

4. It is true that some research indicates that chimpanzees can be taught to communicate with humans and even with fellow chimpanzees by means of nonverbal (gestural) language systems. For example, at the University of Nevada and the University of Oklahoma, it is claimed that chimpanzees have been taught to use portions of the American Sign Language for the deaf (see Eugene Linden, *Apes, Men and Language* [New York: E. P. Dutton, 1974]). If this is the case, then one cannot say that chimpanzees completely lack a rational capacity. But do they have it to the degree necessary to qualify as persons? As impressive as it is that some chimpanzees have managed to learn some of the ASL, there remains an enormous gulf between these chimpanzees and normal adult human beings. If parents were told that a child of theirs would never develop any intellectual ability beyond that achieved by these chimpanzees, none of us would be surprised if they considered it a tragedy. And why a tragedy? Because, I would suggest, in our more frank and honest moments we would acknowledge that the potential for intellectual growth would not be sufficient to enable a full-fledged person to emerge. Further, the claim that apes are capable of language is not beyond dispute (see Herbert Terrance, *Nim: A Chimpanzee Who Learned Sign Language* [New York: Knopf, 1979]).

able, among other things, to comprehend religious ideals, to come to love and cherish those ideals and their embodiment in a Divine Being, to commit our lives to this Being, and so forth. Because we have this capacity, we are able to have personal relationships with each other and with God; because we have this capacity, humans—not animals—have built civilizations and created cultural traditions.

The value we attach to personal agency is in one sense indicated by the fact that we consider an automobile accident that leaves an individual with irreversible brain damage and in a permanently comatose state (i.e., with no chance whatsoever of regaining consciousness) to be a great tragedy. In such cases most of us would conclude that the victim is no longer a person but only a biological organism. Should the comatose individual continue to survive biologically for a long period of time and then die, the death would not strike us as tragic, because what was of real value had already been lost, the tragedy having occurred when the individual's rational capacities were permanently lost. Or consider the case of an anencephalic infant (i.e., an infant born without a cerebral cortex). Such infants invariably die shortly after birth, but if they would continue to live, if we were to perfect and use the skills necessary to keep them alive, they could never engage in any rational activity whatsoever. I would suggest that this is tantamount to saying that personhood would never emerge in them. It is because such infants have no prospect for personal existence that their death does not strike us as tragic. In part it is considerations of this sort that underlie my stipulation that personhood is to be identified with the ability to engage in acts of intellect, emotion, and will at an appropriate level—to exercise, in other words, rational, moral, and spiritual agency. (I shall occasionally refer to this threefold ability simply as personal agency.)

It is helpful to maintain a distinction between the terms *person* and *human*. Although God is a person (as are angels, devils, imaginary beings such as mermaids and satyrs, etc.), he is neither human nor is he a human being. We too are persons but, more precisely, *human* persons; that is, we are persons of the species Homo sapiens. A fetus growing in a woman's womb is human, which is to say that it is not canine, feline, or anything other than human. And a dead corpse is still a *human* corpse even though it is no longer a person, its capacity for rational activity having been irrevocably terminated.[5] So I will be using the term *person* in such a way that an individual can be a person without being human (e.g., God) and an individual can be human without being a person (e.g., a human zygote). Thus, although a fetus is human, it is not a person as we have defined the term, inasmuch as it has not yet developed the functional ability to engage in personal acts.[6]

To be sure, the biological basis for personal life is developing as the fetus grows, but personal life itself does not emerge in the womb at all, nor will it begin to emerge until some time after birth, when the socialization process begins. We rightly acknowledge a fetus to be a potential person, for after a certain period of time and with normal development an individual with rational, moral, and spiritual capacities will normally come into existence. And we rightly acknowledge the newborn to be potential persons as well: they are not yet persons when judged by these strict criteria, for they do not engage in personal acts of intellect, emotion, or will—all that being consequent upon postnatal development. In fact, newborn humans function at a mental level below that of many newborn animals (horses, for example). So if an acquired rational capacity is the mark of personhood, then infants are not persons. Thus whereas both fetuses and newborn infants possess *biological* human life, neither one yet possesses *personal* human life.

---

5. We do speak of "dead persons" but such expressions are not meant to convey the notion that corpses are in fact persons who have the property of being dead. In this regard "dead person" is like "*ex*-ballplayer" and unlike "*good* ballplayer": a good ballplayer is still a ballplayer, but an ex-ballplayer is not. Neither is a "dead person" still a person: it is an ex-person.

6. It should also be noted that when we call an embryo a *human* embryo or a fetus a *human* fetus, we are merely identifying the species to which the embryo or fetus belongs but not affirming that it is a person. Further, I think we should be reluctant to equate either a human embryo or a human fetus with a human being, as many anti-abortionists tend to do, at least at the nonscholarly level of debate. When used as an adjective, the word *human* may simply identify the species of the object it modifies, as in the statement "This is a human fetus." When used as a noun, however, as in the statement "A horse is stronger than a human," it means *human being*. Some people tend in casual speech to slide from a construction such as "This is a human fetus" to "This fetus is a human" to "This fetus is a human being," thinking that because we are justified in using the first construction we are justified in using the second and therefore the third. This is not the case.

This narrow conception of a person, requiring that rationality be actualized before the term *person* is applied, is an admitted stipulation. But it is a stipulation that finds some support in the fact that we come to our conception of a person by looking at paradigmatic cases. In particular, we look at normally functioning adult human beings (and children as well), for there is no doubt whatsoever that these individuals (and all others who possess a similar rational capacity) are persons. We may seek to justify extending this notion, but I know of no unproblematic argument that would *dictate* that human zygotes, for example, be classified as persons. Whatever else may be said, certainly the denial that zygotes are persons is not a contradiction in terms—though neither, I hasten to add, is the affirmation that they are persons. (Interestingly, to say that zygotes *are* persons seems strange to most people, but it also strikes them as strange to say that infants are *not* persons.)

I am proposing, then, that a person is an individual with a developed capacity for rational, moral, and spiritual agency. Admittedly, this is a narrow definition, but it still leaves open the question of whether or not fetuses have a right to life (indeed, one can simply argue that potential persons have a right to life). Further, this definition functions well in helping formulate the fundamental question in the current debate—namely, "What is the connection between personhood in this strict sense and having a right to life?" Three prominent responses have been made to this question: (1) only persons possess a right to life; (2) both (but only) persons and potential persons have a right to life; and (3) all (but only) members of the species Homo sapiens have a right to life—because this is the only species in which persons emerge. We shall subsequently look at all three of these theories and seek to make a judgment about them.

THE IMAGE OF GOD: A STRICT CONSTRUCTION

In a theological context, personhood can be equated with the *imago dei*. That is, to be a finite person is to image God himself. Christian teaching affirms that God is a person and so are we, although he is infinite in character while we are finite. As God engages in acts of intellect, emotion, and will, so do we. In this way we reflect, or image, the divine nature. For my purposes, then, the terms *human person* and *image of God* are virtually synonymous, although the latter term does capture the additional notion that we are finite replicas of God and therefore invested with a special value. Now it may be that the biblical concept of the image of God involves more than our possessing a rational capacity even in this broad sense. It is, for instance, frequently observed that humans image God by ruling over the animal world (Gen. 1:28) and over creation in general, and that in exercising this headship humanity images God, who rules over all things. Nevertheless, it would seem clear that humanity's rational capacity remains fundamental, for without that capacity such headship would be impossible.

As Alan Richardson has observed,

> The Bible makes it clear that there is an essential difference between man and even the highest mammals. It is well aware that man shares with the animals certain characteristics, chief of which is his mortality (cf. Ps. 49:12: "Man is like the beasts that perish"; also Ps. 144:3f.). But he differs from the animals in that God 'visits' him, i.e., holds conversation with him (Ps. 8:4): there is that in man which animals do not possess, namely, man's responsibility before God, the fact that he can answer God's address, hear his law and make or withhold his conscious and deliberate response. There is that in man which is capable of responding to the divine Word; man is akin to God in this respect at least, that he hears God's word: as we say, like speaks to like. . . . To man alone is given the responsibility of conscious choice; man alone of all created things is free to disobey the Creator's will. Thus it is that man alone is conscious of his responsibility before God, is aware that he stands in the presence and under the judgment of God.[7]

Because we are persons, capable of exercising rational, moral, and spiritual agency, we can "answer God's address" and have "responsibility before God," and it is this dimension that the concept of the image of God adds to our previous definition of *person*. It is not so much that our being persons in a universe without God would alter what we were intrinsically—namely, beings capable of personal acts. No, that would remain the same. Rather, it would alter what we *could* be—namely, persons responding to God, knowing him, worshiping him, and being transformed into his moral likeness. Personhood thus takes on special value in a universe with God.

---

7. Richardson, *Genesis I-XI* (London: SCM Press, 1953), pp. 53-54.

Again, I think it is clear from such an understanding of the image of God that in the *strictest* sense it represents, in the same way personhood does, something individuals become rather than something that is instantaneously present before birth or even at birth. Strictly speaking, the image of God emerges after birth as the individual gradually acquires the ability to engage in personal acts to the point of gaining the capacity to "answer God's address" and having "responsibility before God." Infants and fetuses cannot "answer God's address," cannot worship or even so much as comprehend the notion of God, so if being in the image of God is to be actively "imaging" God or to have acquired that capacity, then fetuses and infants are not yet in the image of God. Nor is this a peculiarity that attaches to this particular understanding of the *imago dei*. Indeed, for virtually *any* understanding of the image of God that has found currency in the theological literature, strictly speaking it is not actualized in infants but awaits its realization at a later time with growth and development.[8] But on the other hand, if we move away from a strict construction of what it is to be in the image of God (away, that is, from the contention that it is necessary to actualize the *imago dei* features in one's life), and if instead we adopt a more elastic understanding (that it is sufficient to possess these *imago dei* features only latently, say), then we will be in a position to claim that not only infants but fetuses and newly fertilized ova are in the image of God because they will in due course be imaging God in full actuality.

However, invoking the notion of the image of God is not going to provide a quicker solution to the abortion problem than would otherwise be at our disposal. For when one argues one should argue from the more certain to the less certain, and it does not seem to be any more certain that a fetus is in the image of God than that the fetus has a right to life. Thus, if one could successfully argue *"Infants are in the image of God;* there are no significant differences between infants and fetuses; therefore, fetuses are also in the image of God,"* it would seem no more difficult to argue *"Infants have a right to life;* there are no significant differences between infants and fetuses; therefore, fetuses also have a right to life."*

---

8. For a good survey of the theological literature on the subject of the image of God, see David Cairns, *The Image of God in Man* (London: Collins, 1973).

THE IMAGE OF GOD: NATURE OR STATUS?

It has been argued that it is a mistake to limit the concept of the image of God to human nature—that is, to certain features or characteristics possessed by humans. Clifford E. Bajema notes that

> Some theologians . . . thinking that "image of God" is to be defined *exclusively* in terms of a network of capacities in man, whether latent or expressed, have made the mistake of assuming that if a certain capacity is not ever present (such as the capacity to think as in the case of an anencephalic—one born without a cerbral cortex), then such a one is not in the image of God and is therefore not entitled to the full privileges of the divine image-bearer, such as the right to life under the protection of the sixth commandment ("thou shalt not kill").[9]

Bajema rejects all such definitions on the grounds that they limit the meaning of the image of God to human nature (potential or actualized); he maintains that they must be expanded to include "the dimension of man's *status* (his unique relationship with God through which alone dignity and inviolability are conferred upon him by pure agape love and grace)."[10] Thus, Bajema holds that individuals are valuable not because they have certain capacities (say, the capacity to respond to God and know Him) but solely because they are declared to be valuable by a sovereign act of God: this is what gives them their unique status which in turn calls for special respect by others.

It would seem that Bajema may be doing precisely what he objects to—namely, construing the image of God in such a way that the *nature* and *status* of human beings can be separated. Indeed, his definition tears them asunder. For example, the anencephalic infant, which is by all standards neither actually nor potentially a person since it has no upper brain portion (a light shining in one ear can be seen when looking in the other, the thin membrane which alone provides a barrier glowing brightly), is according to Bajema still in the image of God. As it turns out, Bajema is defining the image of God exclusively in terms of

---

9. Bajema, *Abortion and the Meaning of Personhood* (Grand Rapids: Baker Book, 1974), p. 38. One of these offending theologians referred to by Bajema is the well-known evangelical Anglican John R. W. Stott; see his article "Reverence for Human Life," *Christianity Today* (9 June 1972), pp. 8–12.

10. Bajema, p. 39.

status; he holds that status without nature is sufficient to confer the image of God on an individual (e.g., the anencephalic, who has the status but not the nature)—but apparently that nature without the status would *not* be sufficient. Conceivably God could as easily have conferred his image on apes (who, by the way, have a rational capacity that far exceeds that of the anencephalic) and on other nonpersons as he did on man if, as Bajema suggests, such an act need not entail having to alter their nature at all. God has not done this, of course, but the point is that according to such a view there is no reason why he should not have done so. I do not find this view satisfactory. It is my contention that one's status as a special object of God's love and grace is in fact tied to one's nature as a person (or potential person) who can respond to God, enter into personal relationship with him, and be morally and spiritually accountable to him. It may indeed be, as Christians affirm, that this special status is something *conferred* on persons by God by virtue of his special purposes for them, a status he could have refrained from conferring had he not had those purposes. But it doesn't follow that God confers this status on those without the potential for personal life, who cannot ever participate in those purposes.

THE MORAL AND THE NATURAL IMAGE

Finally, I am inclined to the theological view that the image of God in its fullest sense includes both what has usually been called the "moral image" (holiness) and the "natural image" (rationality, personal agency). The moral image was lost in the Fall, but we retain the natural image—which is to say that we continue to exercise rational, moral, and spiritual agency, although we do so as members of a fallen race and therefore in a sinful and distorted way. However, restoration of the moral image, the object of God's redemptive activity, *presupposes* the existence of the natural image, for it is only personal agents who can be unholy and thus in need of moral and spiritual transformation. If there were no personal agency because no natural image existed, then there could be no possibility of restoring holiness with its concomitant—moral likeness to God.

There are Scripture passages that may reasonably be understood as congruent with this distinction between the moral and the natural image, though I am not so confident as to suggest that these passages actually prove the point I wish to make. Take

Genesis 9:6 for example: "Whoever sheds the blood of man, by man shall his blood be shed; for God made man in his own image." It is possible, contrary to what I am suggesting, to interpret this verse as saying no more than that killing humans is wrong and appropriately punishable only because humans were *originally* made in the image of God, even though that image has been completely lost through the Fall—so that killing Jones, say, is wrong not because *Jones* is in the image of God, but because Jones, although himself not an image-bearer, is a descendant of Adam and thus the descendant of one who was an image-bearer. But surely Genesis 9:6 can also be interpreted with some plausibility to the effect that killing Jones is wrong because Jones is himself an image-bearer, as, indeed, are all descendants of the original image-bearer, they too being made by God and in his image.

Open to the same interpretation is James 3:9—"With it [the tongue] we bless the Lord and Father, and with it we curse men, who are made in the likeness of God." Indeed, a perfectly natural interpretation understands this verse to mean that cursing another human being is wrong because those being cursed are themselves in the likeness of God. So here, too, it is not that cursing Jones represents a fundamental act of disrespect because *Adam* was made in the likeness of God, but because *Jones* is.

At this point an important question arises: What constitutes this likeness to God that Adam and Jones both possess, making both killing and cursing so wrong? The common denominator is not the moral image, because our moral likeness to God has been lost and is in need of restoration (see Rom. 1:18 and 8:7; Eph. 2:1; Col. 1:13). Rather, what suggests itself is precisely what we have been calling the "natural image." This view understands killing and cursing other humans as a failure to respect beings who are special in a certain way—namely, that they image God in their capacity to exercise rational, moral, and spiritual agency, and as a consequence possess, by God's grace, the *possibility* of reflecting the very moral character of God himself.

That a person who sinfully exercises personal agency images God may strike some as strange if not altogether blasphemous. Consequently, they may feel obliged to restrict the application of the term "image of God" to the *proper* exercise of personal agency or to the possession of *sanctified* personal agency. Helmut Thielicke gives quaint expression to this reservation as follows: "Luther declared that if we were to see the *imago Dei* in ontic qualities, we should have to describe the devil as the most perfect image, since he possesses all these qualities in superlative form. The real being of man therefore does not consist in a sum of attributes, but rather in a relationship."[11] But the strangeness of such talk is merely the product of thinking "moral image" (i.e., holiness) instead of "natural image" (i.e., moral agency) when saying "Fallen human beings, the devil included, are in the image of God." It is not being said that fallen humanity (or, for that matter, the devil) images God in the *manner* of exercising personal agency but simply in the fact *that* it is exercised.

THE IMAGE OF GOD: SUMMARY

Thus far we have considered the following principal points:

1. Normal human beings have the capacity to exercise rational, moral, and spiritual agency.

2. In this regard they share a certain kinship with God which makes possible a personal interaction between the two.

3. "Image of God" is an apt term to refer to the human side of this kinship.

4. What is valuable in all human beings is the natural image of God; in possessing this (by God's grace), they possess the potential for imaging God's moral character.

5. The distinction between the natural image of God and the moral image of God is theologically helpful, and it is intimated in Scripture although perhaps not explicitly demonstrable.

If a natural image bearer is one—let us stipulate—who has a *developed* capacity to exercise rational, moral, and spiritual agency, then we are confronted with three main positions on the right to life issue:

Option 1: Only image bearers possess the right to life.

Option 2: Image bearers and potential image bearers possess the right to life.

Option 3: All and only Homo sapiens possess the right to life.

These are the same options set forth in the discussion of "personhood and the right to life." The arguments and implications presented there apply in this context as well. Option 1

---

11. Thielicke, *The Ethics of Sex* (New York: Harper & Row, 1964), p. 31.

yields the conclusion that infants lack the right to life, and that killing infants is therefore not intrinsically objectionable. That conclusion is difficult to accept. Option 3 can be supported along the lines suggested by Bajema (i.e., the image of God is a status conferred by God on all Homo sapiens independently of their capacity for personal existence). This I find unconvincing for the reason already offered—namely, that one's unique status is a product of God's purposes, but these special purposes are possible only for persons and potential persons. My judgment, therefore, favors Option 2 over Option 1 or Option 3. But more about this in subsequent chapters.

FETUSES AND SOULS

Christians (and religious believers in general) are often tempted to think that a determination of whether or not the fetus has a soul would go a considerable way toward resolving the abortion dispute. Presumably, if it could be shown that fetuses do have souls, the resolution would be in favor of a strong anti-abortion position, whereas if it could be shown that fetuses don't have souls, then more liberal options would be open to us. If we remain uncertain whether fetuses have souls, then presumably we will also remain in a quandary over the morality of abortion.

Historically there have been two theories on the origin of the soul. First, there is Creationism, the doctrine that God creates the soul and infuses it in the human form at conception, at birth, or at some point between. Second, there is Traducianism, the theory that the soul is passed on from the parents to the child. Creationism offers a number of possible points at which humans might get souls; Traducians pinpoint the time at the moment of conception.[12] However, may I suggest that for a number of rea-

---

12. Though these are the two traditional views on the matter, we need not feel that in making a final construction we are in any way limited to one or the other. Nor need we accept the view of the soul that these views seem to presuppose—namely, that the soul is the immaterial part of man that is fused into the physical. We might even view the soul simply as the self-conscious agent that emerges following birth, is facilitated by the socialization process, and is dependent upon (though not identical with) the functioning of the brain. As to existence in any interim state between death and resurrection (in which there would be no brain to carry on its consciousness-sustaining activity), we might suppose that God would intervene directly to preserve individual con-

sons reflecting about fetal souls does not help us progress very far on the abortion issue.

Sometimes (though perhaps not in serious discussion by competent theologians) the claim is made that the mere presence of a soul gives an individual his or her special value, along with protection under the sixth commandment. It is not what the soul enables you to do—namely, exercise moral, spiritual, and rational agency—that endows you with this value; rather, there is just something about a soul itself that mysteriously gives you value.[13] This theory suggests that infants (whether normal or anencephalic), adults (whether sleeping or waking), and even fetuses have special value because they all have souls. It also suggests that although we may be impressed with chimpanzee and dolphin intelligence, we can be sure that they don't have souls, and so we can conclude that they lack the right to life.

But this theory does not explain why the possession of a soul endows a being with value. It is hardly an adequate reply to observe that all those to whom we wish to assign a right to life in fact have souls, while all those we are inclined to deny such a right lack souls. To say that all those who have a right to life share a particular property is not to say it is *that* property which endows them with a right to life. It might be that the cell make-up of human tissue is also unique, possessed only by those to whom we are inclined to assign the right to life, but we would not therefore endorse the conclusion that it is that particular feature which endows individuals with a right to life.

Having a soul per se doesn't make one valuable, doesn't make one's life somehow worthy of a special kind of respect. Suppose someone reading these pages lacked a soul but could nevertheless do everything other persons could do. Suppose that although she were soulless she could engage in acts of intellect, emotion, and will, could love God or be indifferent to him, serve him or deny him, worship him or ignore him, and so forth. She

sciousness and the capacity for agency. But this is quite consistent with the view that human beings possess immortality only as God's gift and not simply by virtue of being human. According to such an understanding, however, there is little difference between a soul and the concept of the image of God.

13. Of course to the extent that the soul is *identified* with self-conscious moral and spiritual agency it is not a mystery how souls endow an individual with value: in such a case, the soul would in essence be identical with what is an acknowledged value. But clearly fetuses don't have souls in that sense.

could commit herself to moral and spiritual ideals, do philosophy and theology, have personal relationships with family and friends—all without a soul. It would be quite unconvincing to suggest in the face of this that she were somehow less valuable or that she lacked a right to life or that her life were less worthy of respect than the lives of those who do in fact have souls. H. J. McCloskey makes this point more straightforwardly when he states that "It is possible to deny that man has an immortal soul, without being logically impelled to deny that he may possess rights."[14] For surely what makes a life valuable and worthy of a special respect is this capacity (potential or actualized) to engage in personal acts and be able to "answer God's address," to have "responsibility before God." Further, conservatives on the abortion issue have an interest in affirming McCloskey's point that one need not have a soul in order to have a right to life, for if individuals need a soul in order to have a right to life, then the contention that fetuses have a right to life is no better than the claim that fetuses have souls—which may be very uncertain.

Of course, it might be argued that humans are capable of personal acts *only because* they have souls. That would be to argue that souls have instrumental value (i.e., that they have value because of the things they enable us to do), or in other words that it is good to have a soul because without one we could not do what persons characteristically do. But such a position would not yet establish that the presence of a soul in some mysterious way endows things with value by its mere unfunctioning presence.[15] If there were, for instance, defective souls that could never engage in personal activity, their presence would not endow an individual with the special value we believe attaches to persons. The value of a soul is derivative: it is valuable to have a soul because it makes possible rational, moral, and spiritual agency.

But assume that fetuses do have souls. What would follow from this? The fetal soul would have to be dormant, unless of course we are prepared to say that the unconscious fetus en-

14. McCloskey, "Rights" in *Understanding Moral Philosophy*, ed. James Rachels (Encino: Dickenson, 1976), p. 311.

15. However, it might be suggested that the soul gives us what God also has—a soul-dimension—and thereby endows its possessors with special value, so that it is not a mystery after all. But notice that God's spirit or soul-dimension is significant—surely—only because it enables him to exercise personal agency.

gages in personal activity—and if we know anything, we know that this is not the case. Indeed, as Laura Purdy and Michael Tooley point out, "There are no grounds for believing that the mental life of a human fetus is significantly richer than the mental life of a chimpanzee fetus."[16] Of course it might be insisted that because the fetus has a soul, although dormant, in time it will become a person in the full sense, engaging in acts of intellect, emotion, and will. But this doesn't tell us anything relevant to the abortion dispute that we don't already know; it is already clear that fetuses will, after the normal course of development, mature into persons and exercise rational agency. While it might be that the initial infusing of a soul in a fetus would represent a significant step toward the ultimate realization of personhood, still it might well be argued in response that such growth toward personhood could be better measured by assessing neurological development than by speculating about fetal souls and their development.

But none of this should be surprising to biblically oriented Christians, who hold that it is the concept of the image of God and not the concept of having a soul that is central to valuing human beings and differentiating them from nonhuman animals. I do not wish to deny that persons have a nonmaterial dimension to them and that this is in part what we refer to when we use the terms "soul," "spirit," and "mind." Nevertheless, it is our capacity to exercise moral, spiritual, and intellectual agency that should be at the fore of our thinking when we confront the abortion question and in general when we seek to focus on what it is that gives human beings their special value. When we seek to place a value on the human fetus, it is its unique potential for personal agency, its potential for imaging God and not the presence or absence of a nonmaterial component to its being that should receive primary attention. This is true for at least two reasons: first, it reflects an appropriate theological and biblical priority, and second, it avoids the mystery and uncertainty involved in speculation about fetal souls.

ABORTION AND THE IMMORTALITY OF THE SOUL

If the fetus has an *immortal* soul that will suffer a terrible postmortem fate should it be killed by an act of abortion, then

---

16. Purdy and Tooley, "Is Abortion Murder?" in *Abortion: Pro and Con*, ed. Robert L. Perkins (Cambridge: Schenkman, 1974), p. 133.

that would be a consideration of overwhelming importance to the current debate. Glanville Williams has claimed that "The historical reason for the Catholic objection to abortion is the same as for the Christian Church's historical opposition to infanticide: the horror of bringing about the death of an unbaptized child. Dying in original sin without the sacrament of baptism, the child is condemned to eternal punishment."[17]

Whether this is historically correct or not—and there may be reason to doubt that it is[18]—still, it refers to a contention that, if true, would justify a moral ban on virtually all abortions. Indeed, as W. E. H. Lecky has noted, "The criminality of abortion was immeasurably aggravated when it was believed to involve, not only the extinction of transient life, but also the damnation of an immortal soul."[19]

The first thing to notice, by way of a Christian response, is that souls are not immortal by virtue of some property intrinsic to them.[20] If there is existence beyond the grave, the Christian

---

17. Williams, *The Sanctity of Life and the Criminal Law* (New York: Alfred A. Knopf, 1972), p. 193. W. E. H. Lecky states that "to the theologian this infant life possessed a fearful significance. The moment, they taught, the fetus in the womb acquired animation, it became an immortal being, destined, even if it died unborn, to be raised again on the last day, responsible for the sin of Adam, and doomed, if it perished without baptism, to be excluded forever from heaven and to be cast, as the Greeks taught, into painless and joyless limbo, or, as the Latins taught, into the abyss of hell. It is probably, in a considerable degree, to this doctrine that we owe in the first instance the healthy sense of the value and sanctity of infant life which so broadly distinguishes Christian from pagan societies, and which is now so thoroughly incorporated with our moral feelings as to be independent of all doctrinal changes" (*History of European Morals* [New York: D. Appleton, 1870], 2: 23).

18. One such doubter is John T. Noonan, Jr. See his essay "An Almost Absolute Value in History," in *The Morality of Abortion*, ed. John T. Noonan, Jr. (Cambridge: Harvard University Press, 1970), p. 51.

19. Lecky, 2: 23.

20. The argument that souls are intrinsically immortal is essentially non-Christian. One such argument (perhaps hinted at by Plato in the *Phaedo* and endorsed by certain pagan philosophers after him) proceeds as follows: Souls have the property of being absolutely simple, which is to say that they have no parts whatsoever and thus cannot be divided or torn asunder. And because it was held that the only way to destroy a thing is to tear it asunder, bringing a halt to its functioning by dividing its parts, it was concluded that a soul could not be destroyed even by the passage of time, and so it could never perish. Indeed, it was maintained that not even God could destroy a soul, that it would be logically impossible for him to do so: you can't tear apart what has no parts. Thus, once a soul is brought into existence, this argument held, it will continue

maintains it is only because God chooses to sustain us in our existence and not because we have souls that are in and of themselves immortal. Only Christ has immortality (1 Tim. 6:16) and we have it, the Christian community claims, as his gift. Furthermore, we have no biblical grounds for the belief that God will choose to sustain the existence of fetal souls (assuming that there are such things). All talk of postmortem existence for fetal souls is at best theological speculation. It follows from this that we have no reason to believe that there is any portmortem existence for fetal souls, let alone that there is an *horrendous* postmortem existence in store for them. Consequently, it would be gratuitous to make an abortion decision based on such a possibility.

Nevertheless, aborted fetuses, anencephalic infants, normal infants who die in infancy, and the excessively retarded do pose for the Christian a painful theological problem. As Austin Farrer has put it,

> We do not know how we should relate to the mercy of God beings who never enjoy a glimmer of reason. Are they capable of eternal salvation or are they not? ... The baby smiled before it died. Will God bestow immortality on a smile? Shall we say that every human birth, however imperfect, is the germ of personality, and that God will give it an eternal future? We shall still have to ask why the fact of being born should be allowed a decisive importance; we shall wonder what of children dying in the womb or suffering abortion; and we shall be at a loss where to draw the line. Not that it will be any easier to draw it if we equate the origin of an immortal soul with the attainment of speech or reason. For we shall still have to ask, What degree of reason? Rationality comes by stages in those who acquire it, and not all imbeciles are totally mindless. ... We do not know where to draw the line; that is to say, we do not know where God draws it.[21]

The problem is posed for us because in each of these cases (fetuses, infants, the massively retarded) there is no personal life and consequently no "person" that can be preserved beyond the grave. There is no personality, no character, no mind that can be restored in some postmortem state. Christian belief may in-

---

to exist forever. (See A. E. Taylor, *Plato* [New York: World Publishing, 1961], p. 189.)

21. Farrer, *Love Almighty and Ills Unlimited* (Garden City, N.Y.: Doubleday, 1961), p. 166.

deed affirm that a radical transformation takes place as an individual enters into the fullness of eternal life, but presumably there remains a recognizable continuity between the premortem and postmortem individual. Mental abilities may well be heightened, character purified, and personality improved, but what existed before death is not eradicated or annihilated, surely, so that some new discontinuous individual might emerge. After all, we are supposed to recognize people in heaven and—perhaps even more importantly—to recognize ourselves. But we would not recognize this former fetus or former infant, and neither would a former fetus or infant be capable of self-recognition. Such an individual would simply, all of a sudden, exist as a full-fledged person for the first time.

A further complication confronts us. In directly bestowing immortality upon a fetus or an infant, God would be creating *ex nihilo* an individual who loves him without ever having come to love him, who is committed to Christ without ever having made a commitment to him, who possesses values or ideals without ever having chosen them, who has a personality without ever having developed it, who has knowledge without ever having sought it, and so forth. One may wonder what the point of historical existence is if all this can be done by an automatic and instantaneous metamorphosis. To the extent that we hold that historical existence has a point because it provides us with the opportunity to make certain critical choices and commitments that determine our ultimate destiny, then to that extent we will have to be uncomfortable with the suggestion that there is postmortem existence for fetuses and the like. Once again we are confronted with the problem of determining the sense in which this metamorphosed individual is the same being as the fetus. To be sure, we might posit the existence of a propertyless spiritual substratum in the fetus (a perplexing notion in its own right) and then claim that after death God subsequently takes that substratum and invests it with the properties of a sanctified, full-fledged person. But notice that this is not the preservation of a person; rather, it is the preservation of a characterless substratum used to create a person in heaven. Further, we might also wonder why God would not simply place this characterless spiritual substratum in another fetus and give it the opportunity to experience historical existence. The same problem emerges whether we are speaking of a newly fertilized ovum, a developed fetus, an infant (normal or anencephalic), or the massively retarded. On this matter, I am not aware of any clear teaching in Scripture, so I feel there is reason for justified uncertainty.[22] Austin Farrer's comments are once more appropriate:

> We may be sure that he [God] loves and saves whatever is there to be saved or loved; if his love or power does not act, it is because there is nothing for it to act upon. . . . But there is no certain light on this painful matter; nor is there any honesty in dogmatizing where we have nothing to go upon.[23]

So the uncertainty on this issue is real. In any case, though, for our present purposes it doesn't matter what response one makes, since the whole point is irrelevant to the abortion dispute. What is relevant is not whether the fetus, the normal infant, or the anencephalic infant will have personal existence in the *next* life but only whether they can have it in *this* life. Many who count themselves Christians believe otherwise, feeling that the knowledge that we are dealing with an individual who has an eternal destiny will heighten our respect for the life in our hands sufficiently to incline us to pro-life decisions. But notice that when considering whether or not to unplug a life-support system keeping a brain-damaged adult alive, what we need desperately to know is not what postmortem expectation the patient might have but what the possibilities of continued personal existence *in this life* might be. However firm our conviction might be that this individual shall, by God's provision, live again beyond the grave, we do not hold it to be a determining factor in

---

22. A Scripture passage often used to comfort parents who have lost an infant and to affirm the prospect of a postmortem reunion is found in II Samuel 12:23. These are words spoken by David after the death of his own infant son: "But now he is dead, wherefore should I fast? Can I bring him back again? I shall go to him, but he shall not return to me." But most likely David was simply thinking that he too would one day die and go into the grave, joining his infant son in that sense. Hans Hertzberg's comment is characteristic of biblical commentators: "David's statement that he cannot bring the child back but must in the end go to him is no expression of hope in a future life, but simply of the immutability of death" (*I and II Samuel: A Commentary*, trans. J. A. Bowden, Old Testament Library [1964; Philadelphia: Westminster Press, 1965], p. 316). See also G. B. Caird, "I and II Samuel," in *The Interpreter's Bible*, ed. George Arthur Buttrick et al. (New York: Abingdon-Cokesbury Press, 1951-57), 2: 1106; John Mauchline, *I and II Samuel*, New Century Bible (London: Oliphants, 1971), p. 256; and D. F. Payne, "1 and 2 Samuel," in *The New Bible Commentary*, 3d ed. rev., ed. Donald Guthrie and J. A. Motyer (Grand Rapids: William B. Eerdmans, 1970), p. 307.

23. Farrer, pp. 167-68.

our deliberation. Why should we act differently in considering
the possibility of an abortion or suspending heroic life-saving
efforts for an infant. That the fetus (or infant) has an eternal
destiny may give it special value, but it is not a value relevant to
our decision-making. On the other hand, the fact that the fetus
or infant has a potential for personhood in this life *is* a consideration that we ought to take into account. We may rightly make
a pro-life decision based on that consideration alone even if we
are fully persuaded that aborted fetuses (or infants) have no
postmortem prospect.

In conclusion, then, I would like to suggest that the question
of whether fetuses have immortal souls is essentially irrelevant
to the abortion debate. Such a consideration would be relevant
only if the act of abortion were also an act of damnation—a
contention that has no support in the biblical tradition. What is
most relevant is the prospect for personal existence in this life,
and the full value of that consideration can be appreciated independently of any belief in a postmortem existence for aborted
fetuses.

SUMMARY

The conclusions we have reached in this chapter are basically negative but nonetheless important. The abortion debate, I
have argued, cannot be settled simply by defining the term
person so that it includes newly fertilized ova, thereby giving to
the human conceptus full moral standing. Nor can matters be
settled by defining *person* so that it excludes fetuses, thereby
denying moral status to the unborn. The debate simply cannot
be won by legislating definitions. In both cases the definitions
would be stipulations, neither of which would be clearly more
reasonable than the other. So as a way of proceeding I have
chosen to define *person* very narrowly, restricting its scope to
include only those who have an actualized capacity for personal
agency and rationality, thus excluding fetuses and infants as
persons. This definition settles nothing; it only serves to raise the
question of whether potential persons have a right to life. Clearly
there is a widespread, strong conviction that infants, who are
"only" potential persons, do have a right to life. It may be that
the potential for personhood in some sense invests one with a
right to life. We sense that it does so in the case of infants, so
why not in the case of fetuses? Conservatives need not object to

this narrow definition of personhood, since it still leaves them in a good position to make their anti-abortion case. But argument is, of course, required.

These comments about determining the outcome of the abortion debate by stipulative definition also apply to the concept of the image of God. We cannot settle matters by defining *image of God* in such a way that it covers all fetal life. For matters here are genuinely controversial. Are human zygotes in the image of God or are they not? There are not, I have suggested (and will continue to suggest), any decisive arguments to answer this question with sufficient certainty to settle the abortion question. Even if we were to determine that fetuses are not in the image of God, we would not yet have determined that those with a natural potential for imaging God did not have a right to life. It might very well be that potential image bearers have a right to life. If we could establish this, we might then proceed to conclude that because those who have a natural potential for actively imaging God also have a right to life, it is appropriate to declare further that they are in the image of God. Indeed when it comes to relating such terms as *person* or *image of God* to the abortion debate, we may choose not to argue "Fetuses are persons in the image of God; therefore, fetuses possess a right to life" but rather that "Fetuses possess a right to life; therefore, fetuses are persons in the image of God."

How we apply significant terms ought not to be the critical premise from which our conclusion is to follow; rather, how we apply these terms ought to be the all-important conclusion that we reach after the debate is over. It would be more fitting to conclude that an individual (e.g., a fetus) who has a unique potential for imaging God (though it is not yet actualized) and also has a right to life is therefore a bearer of the divine image, a person, than to presume the converse. But in the meantime, as we carry on the debate, I shall hold to a narrow definition of both *person* and *image bearer*, assuming that the terms refer only to those individuals with an actualized capacity to exercise personal agency.

In discussing fetal souls, I have argued for two conclusions: first, that the existence of such souls is problematic, and second, that there is no conceptual connection between having a soul and having a right to life. That one has no soul, in other words, does not entail that one has no right to life, just as having a soul does not necessarily guarantee that one has a right to life. Discussing the nature of fetal souls is not, then, a good way to make progress on the question. Nor is the notion of possessing a soul the biblical way to affirm the value of human life. More appropriate from a biblical and theological standpoint is the concept of the image of God.

4

Establishing
a Right to Life:
Decisive Moment Theories

Most abortion theories claim that there is a particular moment in time when there comes into existence a being that has a full-fledged right to life. It is presumed that there is a critical occurrence, usually abrupt and decisive, prior to which there is not a human being (or a person) with a right to life and after which there is. Growth and development may be required to get to that point, but there does come a time when the line is crossed and one enters into possession of the right to life fully and completely. Some theories hold that there is a gray area in which it is not clear whether the line has been crossed. The larger the gray area, of course, the more uncertainty and ambiguity one introduces into the abortion question.

Such views, which we might call "decisive moment" theories, stand in contrast to "gradualist" theories, which claim that becoming a human being, or a person, or a holder of a strong right to life is a gradual process occurring over a more extended period of time, and that personhood, or humanity, or the strength of one's right to life is a matter of degree. Decisive moment theories do not talk in terms of degree but in terms of either/or; they presume that at a given moment one either has the right to life completely or lacks it altogether.

There are a number of different decisive moment theories, each specifying a different point at which one acquires totally one's status as a person with the attendant right to life. Some theories hold that the decisive occurrence is prenatal, occurring at the moment of conception, or when the zygote implants in the uterine wall, or when the fetus achieves viability, external human form, or adequate brain development. Other theories hold that the decisive moment occurs at the point of birth, or when personal consciousness emerges. Some of the theories lend themselves to both gradualist and decisive moment interpretations. One could argue, for instance, that as the brain and central nervous system develop and grow so does the right to life, but one could also argue that as soon as brain waves can be recorded there is an individual with a full-fledged right to life—and not before. However, in our initial look at these theories we shall view them all as decisive moment theories.

DECISIVE MOMENT THEORY ONE: CONCEPTION

Of all the decisive moment theories, the one that presumes the human fetus to have an absolute right to life from the point of conception is the most conservative and, in many ways, the most straightforward. In the public mind, it is associated with the official teaching of the Roman Catholic Church, though it is held by others as well, including many conservative Protestants and even secularists. The claim is that at the point of human conception, when the female ovum is fertilized by the male sperm, there comes into existence a being that merits the same full respect that is due any person. It would seem to follow, and is often so argued, that virtually none of the reasons prompting women to seek abortions is in fact adequate to justify such acts. After all, we don't kill *children* who are unwanted, or deformed, or retarded, or the product of rape, or who stand in the way of our career opportunities, or are the source of our psychological problems, or constitute a financial liability. We would not condone killing children under such circumstances even if there were no apparent alternative solutions to these problems. The reason we hold such a view is that we consider children to be persons, each with a person's right to life that ought to be respected and not set aside for the kinds of reasons just given. But if a fetus also has a person's right to life, then abortion must be invariably—and seriously—wrong. An abortion might possibly be justified to save the mother's life, but even that is not beyond dispute given the premise of an absolute right to life from conception.

The Argument from Genetic Endowment

The appeal to genetic endowment is not merely the contention that the zygote (a newly fertilized ovum) is a living organism, for so are the ovum and the sperm *prior* to fertilization, and no one is interested in claiming that ova and sperm are human beings or that the use of artificial birth control is a serious act of killing. (The Roman Catholic Church in its official teaching may condemn the use of artificial contraception, but it does not do so for the same reasons it condemns abortion; abortion may involve something akin to murder according to the church's view, but artificial birth control involves only an illicit interruption in a natural process.) The critical difference between the zygote and either the ovum or sperm is that in the case of the zygote the genetic determinants of the subsequent individual are built into the organism in the form of the genetic code. "These include the features of the human species and also the individual trademarks such as male or female sex, the color of eyes, hair and skin; the configuration of face and body; the tendency to be tall or short, fat or lean, ruggedly healthy or prone to some diseases; and undoubtedly also the tendency to certain qualities of termperament and intelligence."[1] Thus, the future human being is latent in the zygote to an extent to which it is not latent in the ovum or sperm. For the first time, with the fertilization of the ovum, we can point to a single living organism in which there is contained encoded instructions for the subsequent unfolding of the whole organism. As one defender of the present view has put it, speaking of the conceptus, "From the very beginning it is visibly impelled by a goal-oriented impetus—and that goal is exclusively human."[2]

What the argument from genetic endowment establishes is that from the moment of conception there exists the natural potential for personhood, which is to say that in time the unique potential in the zygote will (with a certain degree of probability) unfold and a person will emerge. But this merely raises the question of whether "potential persons" have the same strong

1. Geraldine Lux Flanagan, *The First Nine Months of Life* (New York: Simon & Schuster, 1962), p. 32.

2. David Granfield, *The Abortion Decision* (Garden City, N.Y.: Image Books, 1971), p. 38.

right to life as actual persons. Thus, the appeal to genetic endowment establishes the zygote's special potential, but it does not tell us what significance we should assign to that potential. In order to do that we must turn to the argument from potentiality.

The Appeal to Potentiality

How does one support the claim that whatever has a natural potential for personhood also has a right to life—the same strong right to life that adult human beings have? One might search for examples of individuals who undeniably have a right to life but who could have that right to life only by virtue of their potential or prospect for personhood. If such examples could be found, they would provide substantial support for the claim that potentiality for personhood invests one with a right to life, and thus that fetuses have a right to life. Perhaps infants would serve the purpose. Certainly most people would concur that infants have a right to life and that their lives ought to be held inviolate—and it might well be argued that they have that right to life or inviolate status because they are biologically human life on the way to becoming personal human life. That much established, it could be argued that there is no substantial difference between the fetus and the infant: the fetus, too, is biological life on the way to becoming personal human life; it merely lags behind the infant by a few months. Although a fetus cannot think, exercise moral or spiritual agency, have hopes or aspirations for the future, or do any of the things that a fully developed human being can do, neither can the infant. The value of the infant, then, is grounded not in what it has actualized but in what it has the potential to actualize, and since fetuses share this potential, they should also share the infant's status and possess a right to life.

This is an interesting and, I believe, powerful argument. But we must postpone giving it a full examination until we have examined the potentiality principle (along with its competitors, the actuality principle and the species principle) in greater detail. That complications await us is intimated by the fact that *unfertilized* ova also have a potential (in some sense) for developing into persons, and yet we are not inclined to suppose that they have a right to life. What needs to be explained is why the potential possessed by the fertilized ova confers a right to life but the potential possessed by the unfertilized ova does not. Further, the

potential for personhood that we see in the infant represents a
level of neurophysiological development not present in a zygote
or embryo; among other things, the infant has a brain, whereas
a newly fertilized ovum does not. We may well wonder whether
this advanced level of development does not provide some basis
for distinguishing the moral status of infants from the moral
status of zygotes.

The Benefit of the Doubt Argument

It has been argued that uncertainty over the moral status of
the zygote (and embryo and fetus) favors the conservative position. The conservative might very well concede that it has not
been demonstrated that the zygote has the same claim to life as
individuals who undeniably are persons while also pointing out
that it has not been conclusively demonstrated that the zygote
has no such right. The fact is that we just don't know which is
the case. So, the argument continues, we ought to play it safe
and act as if the zygote were endowed with the same right to
life that we persons possess, lest we unwittingly violate a right
to life.[3] Of course this argument will call for adopting a hard line
on the abortion issue; in effect it calls for us to act as if abortion
were as serious as murder. While it doesn't try to establish that
killing fetuses is a moral equivalent to murder, it does suggest
that the very possibility must be avoided at all costs.

To all of this, however, there is another side. A twist can be
given to this kind of argument that will yield liberal implications
on the abortion question. One might begin with the claim that
we don't know the moral status of the fetus and conclude that
we don't know that aborting zygotes is murder. But one might
then make the point that we do know that considerable value
attaches to meeting the needs of a pregnant girl or woman. Here
no complicated argumentation or metaphysical speculation is
called for. To help a person avoid pain, emotional scars, psychological problems, economic stress is good and we know it to be
good. One might then argue that it is unreasonable to turn our

---

3. This argument can be formulated in two basic ways: in terms of
uncertainty about whether a fetus is a person, or in terms of uncertainty about
the moral status of the fetus (i.e., uncertainty about whether potential persons
have as strong a right to life as fully actualized persons).

back on known goods (the reduction of human suffering) in order to avoid what we do not know to be evil (aborting a fetus).

Consider the following case. A thirty-six-year-old woman with four children, worn down and exhausted by poverty and terrible living conditions, married to an alcoholic husband finds herself pregnant. Although not the sole source of income for her family, the woman does work and her income is desperately needed. After wrestling with her predicament, the woman decides that an abortion would be in the interests of herself and of her family. She is convinced of this by the same considerations that prompted her to take birth control measures to begin with—measures that in this instance failed. Concerned about whether abortion might be the killing of a being with a right to life, she consults two moralists, both of whom appeal to the Benefit of the Doubt Argument. One is a "conservative" who warns her to avoid the possibility of a great moral evil—terminating the life of what *might* be a holder of a right to life. The other is a "liberal" who encourages her to secure what she *knows* to be good—avoiding considerable suffering for herself and her family.

It seems to me that both pieces of advice are reasonable and that neither is clearly superior to the other. The conservative stresses the *magnitude* of the moral evil to be avoided by not having an abortion; the liberal stresses the certainty of the suffering to be avoided by having an abortion. So it would seem that the less sure one is that the fetus is a bearer of a right to life and the greater the burden that can be avoided by having an abortion, the more one would be inclined to favor a liberal decision and proceed with an abortion. On the other hand, the more certain one is that the fetus is a bearer of a right to life and the lighter the burden that can be avoided by having an abortion, the more one would be inclined to favor a conservative decision. Thus it turns out that our judgment will depend on how uncertain one is about the moral status of the fetus (which will vary from person to person) and how great a burden can be avoided by having an abortion (which will vary from pregnancy to pregnancy). The upshot of this is that the Benefit of the Doubt Argument does not always succeed in settling matters in favor of the conservative, although it may for some people in some circumstances.

The Biblical Argument

There are a number of standard Scripture passages that are often invoked to support the claim that conception is the divinely indicated juncture that marks the beginning of personal existence with its attendant right to life. Among them are the following:

For thou didst form my inward parts,
    thou didst knit me together in my mother's womb.
I praise thee, for thou art fearful and wonderful.
    Wonderful are thy works!
Thou knowest me right well;
    my frame was not hidden from thee,
when I was being made in secret,
    intricately wrought in the depths of the earth.
Thy eyes beheld my unformed substance;
    in thy book were written, every one of them,
the days that were formed for me,
    when as yet there was none of them. (Psalm 139:13-16)

Before I formed you in the womb I knew you,
and before you were born I consecrated you;
I appointed you a prophet to the nations. (Jeremiah 1:5)

After surveying these and a few other verses (Luke 1:44; Ps. 1:5), Harold O. J. Brown was sufficiently certain to declare forthrightly that "There can be no doubt that God clearly says the unborn child is already a human being, made in the image of God and deserving of protection under the law."[4] But it seems to me that Brown is a bit overconfident. For what is at issue here is not whether these biblical affirmations support a strong respect for developing human life—of course they do—but whether they support the theory that at exactly the moment of fertilization, not before and not after, there comes into existence an individual who has a right to life identical with that of the reader or writer of these words.

These verses certainly declare that it is God whose creative activity is at work in the womb forming the individual.[5] This is

---

4. Brown, *Death before Birth* (Nashville: Thomas Nelson, 1977), p. 127.
    5. It ought, incidentally, to be noted that to maintain that God is at work in the womb is not to deny any biological realities (e.g., the sperm fertilizing the ovum and creating the zygote), for these can be viewed as the secondary means through which God works his will and purposes.

impressive, awe-inspiring, and not without implications for our attitude toward life, but by itself it does not establish that a newly fertilized ovum has a person's claim to life, nor does it constitute grounds for a strict moral prohibition of abortion. For notice that the passages do not confine God's creative activity to the period that begins with conception; they describe him as also being active in the process preceding conception. But if it is God's creative activity that confers a right to life, then a right to life must exist prior to conception. That conclusion would entail that the employment of artificial contraception is as problematic as abortion unless we could find some way to argue that the divine activity after fertilization is somehow different than the divine activity before fertilization.

Harold Brown also contends that "It is abundantly clear from Scripture that God relates to us and is personally concerned for us before birth." Why, we may ask, is this significant? Brown states that "If God relates in a personal way to a human creature this is evidence that that creature is made in God's image."[6] But I would contend that his argument trades on an ambiguity. To be *personally concerned* with another before birth (as an expectant mother might have her own personal concerns that her baby will be strong and healthy at birth and grow up to be an adult of good character) is not the same as being *personally related* to another (the woman cannot have a person-to-person relationship with a newly fertilized ovum). If God were *personally related* to an individual, that would be an undeniable sign of the presence of the image of God in that individual, but we have no real evidence that God, any more than the woman, has a person-to-person relationship with a single-cell zygote. Again, we do have ample evidence from Scripture that God is personally *concerned* with individuals not only before their *birth* but before their *conception;* as he declares in the oft-quoted Jeremiah 1:5, *"Before* I formed you in the womb I knew you...." But the fact remains that God's knowing Jeremiah before his conception does not demonstrate the presence of the image of God at that early point. If it did, artificial contraception would be as problematic as abortion.

Brown also uses Scripture less than persuasively when he seeks to generalize from an account involving the unborn John

---

6. Brown, p. 126.

the Baptist.[7] In the passage in question, Mary greets Elizabeth, who has come to visit her, and "when Elizabeth heard the greetings of Mary, the babe leaped in her womb" (Luke 1:41). Elizabeth subsequently interprets the event as follows: "When the voice of your greeting came to my ears, the babe in my womb leaped for joy" (Luke 1:44). This interpretation can be viewed as an example of legitimate poetic license or even as the reporting of a miraculous sign. Brown assumes the latter, suggesting that the fetal John the Baptist recognized the presence of the fetal Jesus and then rejoiced over it. But it is clearly bad methodology to generalize from such an atypical circumstance. Surely one would not want to maintain that all fetuses are capable of such acts of cognition in the womb—capable, that is, of comprehending certain facts ("This is the Messiah") and then experiencing a range of emotional responses to what they comprehend. Nevertheless, even if this passage does not establish that the unborn are persons, we should acknowledge that, along with the other stories associated with the birth of Jesus, it does serve to underscore the fact that the unborn are special, ringed around with a sacredness that must be respected. It would be difficult to reflect on the nativity stories devotionally and remain indifferent to such practices as infanticide and abortion. I think we can safely say that Brown has articulated an abortion theory that is consistent with the biblical emphasis—but this is not to say that it is the *only* theory consistent with that emphasis.

Brown also argues that Scripture recognizes that an individual's identity begins with conception. He cites, for example, the Psalmist's declaration that, "Behold, I was brought forth in iniquity, and in sin did *my* mother conceive me" (Ps. 51:5). There are other verses (e.g., Ps. 139:13, 15) in which developing fetal life is likewise referred to with personal pronouns. But again, such references designate individuals not only before birth but before conception (e.g., Jer. 1:5: "*Before* I formed *you* in the womb I knew *you*"), and so they are not really to the point. As one able church study document has put it, "The use of these personal pronouns does not prove that those in the womb are, while in the womb, persons. That use proves only that in God's plan those particular fetuses were (at least) destined to become persons."[8] And they were so destined even before conception.

---

7. See Brown, p. 127.

8. Orthodox Presbyterian Church, "Report of the Committee to Study the Matter of Abortion" (May 1971), p. 12.

Extending our examination, it would be a mistake to argue that since it was David who *was being formed* in his mother's womb (Ps. 51:5) it must therefore have been David *the person* who was in his mother's womb. That would be to confuse the "formation/creation" of a thing with the "completion/existence" of that thing. The fact is that an entity can be on the way to becoming a particular thing without it being that thing. It is quite natural for us to refer to what is in the process of becoming (the zygote or fetus in a Semite woman's womb) in terms of what it will eventually become (a King David), but we are not then speaking with technical accuracy. If a butterfly *is being formed* in a cocoon, it does not follow that there *is* a butterfly there (rather than a caterpillar or something betwixt or between). In this connection the following comments demonstrate a sensitivity to language:

> If the fetus were not a person from conception, it is not clear that the writers would have avoided the personal pronouns. In Psm. 139:13 and in Psm. 51:5, David is reflecting on his origins. . . . In considering his relation with God, [he] traces it back to his fetal life, back even to his conception. Naturally, he uses the terms "me" and "my"; the use of "it," whether more precise or not, would be jarring, pedantic and pointless. These pronouns are quite natural even on the supposition that the unborn child is *not* a person from conception. . . . If the fetus were not a person from conception, it is not clear that the writers would have avoided the personal pronouns.[9]

These verses, then, do not teach—either directly or by implication—that the zygote or fetus is a person, an individual fully in the image of God. Nor do they teach that zygotes have the same claim to life as a person. As one reads these verses one cannot help but receive the impression that fetal life is to be respected, valued, honored—but this does not by itself translate neatly into a full and unqualified right-to-life-from-conception position.

The Argument from Exodus 21:22–25

The closest Scripture comes to dealing directly with the abortion issue is in a reference in the Old Testament law code to accidentally induced miscarriage:

---

9. "Report of the Committee to Study the Matter of Abortion," p. 12.

> When men strive together, and hurt a woman with child, so that there is a miscarriage, and yet no harm follows, the one who hurt her shall be fined, according as the woman's husband shall lay upon him; and he shall pay as the judges determine. If any harm follows, then you shall give life for life, eye for eye, tooth for tooth, hand for hand, foot for foot, burn for burn, wound for wound, stripe for stripe. (Ex. 21:22-25 RSV)

The passage is sufficiently ambiguous to divide interpreters. Some critics hold that the fetus and the woman are treated according to different principles, a different status being ascribed to each.[10] If the woman is caused to miscarry but is not herself injured, then those who cause the miscarriage are to pay the husband compensation for the loss of his property (i.e., the fetus), but if the *woman* dies or is injured then the principle of *lex talionis* applies (i.e., an eye for an eye, etc.). According to this interpretation, accidentally killing a fetus is not as serious as accidentally killing a woman. The fetus has the status of property, whereas the woman receives the full protection of the law governing persons. This interpretation is made explicit in the American Bible Society's Today's English Version:

> If some men are fighting and hurt a pregnant woman so that she loses her child, but she is not injured in any other way, the one who hurt her is to be fined whatever amount the woman's husband demands, subject to the approval of the judges. But if the woman herself is injured, the punishment shall be life for life. . . .

This interpretation is disputed, however. Other critics argue that the *lex talionis* covers both the woman and the fetus, giving them equality of treatment under the law.[11] One commentator

---

10. Among those holding this view are Ronald E. Clements (*Exodus*, Cambridge Commentaries on the New English Bible [Cambridge: Cambridge University Press, 1972], p. 138), J. Philip Hyatt (*Exodus*, New Century Bible [London: Oliphants, 1971], p. 233), Martin Noth (*Exodus: A Commentary*, trans. J. S. Bowden [1959; Philadelphia: Westminster Press, 1962], p. 181), and J. Coert Rylaarsdam ("Exodus," in *The Interpreter's Bible*, ed. George Arthur Buttrick et al. [New York: Cokesbury-Abingdon Press, 1951-57], 1: 999).

11. Among those holding this view are C. F. Keil and F. Delitzsch ("The Second Book of Moses: Exodus," in *The Pentateuch*, vol. 1 of *Commentary on the Old Testament* [1864-1901; rpt., Grand Rapids: William B. Eerdmans, 1980], p. 135) and Umberto Cassuto (*A Commentary on the Book of Exodus*, trans. Israel Abrahams [Jerusalem: Magnes Press, 1967], p. 275).

who shares this point of view makes the following interpretative remarks:

> The statute commences, *And when men strive together,* etc., in order to give an example of accidental injury to a pregnant woman, and . . . the law presents the case realistically. Details follow: *and they hurt* unintentionally *a woman with child* —the sense is, that one of the combatants, whichever of them it be (for this reason the verb translated 'and they hurt' is in the plural) is responsible—*and her children come forth* (i.e., there is a miscarriage) on account of the hurt she suffers (irrespective of the nature of the fetus, be it male or female, one or two; hence here, too, there is a generic plural as in the case of the verb 'they hurt'), *but no mischief happens*—that is, the woman and the children do not die—the one who hurt her *shall surely be punished* by a fine, *according as the woman's husband shall lay*—impose—*upon him,* having regard to the extent of the injuries and the special circumstances of the accident; *and he* who caused the hurt *shall pay* the amount of the fine to the woman's husband *with judges,* in accordance with the decision of the court that will confirm the husband's claim and compel the offender to pay compensation, for it is impossible to leave the determination of the amount of the fine to the husband, and, on the other hand, it is not within the husband's power to compel the assailant to pay if he refuses. But if *any mischief happen,* that is, if the woman dies or the children die, *then you shall give life for life,* eye for eye, etc.: you, O judge (or you, O Israel, through the judge who represents you) shall adopt the principle of "life for life," etc.[12]

There are then difficulties standing in the way of using the Exodus 21:22-25 passage in the abortion debate. First, the interpretation of the passage is disputed, based on genuine ambiguities in the text and not simply reflecting the biases of interpreters. Second, even if we could be certain of our interpretation, we might well still be uncertain about what general lessons could be extracted from the passage. It could be argued that the laws laid down in Exodus 21 and 22 are contextual in nature and not generalizable to other times and places (note that bestiality is punishable by death according to Ex. 22:19, but there is no punishment for one who strikes his slave and causes him to die a day or two later according to Ex. 21:21). At the very least

---

12. Cassuto, p. 275.

one would have to think this through very carefully before making any applications to the current abortion dispute.

The Appeal to the Continuum

Some would contend that as we move back in time from birth to conception there is no discernible difference from moment to moment—that is, there is no difference between an infant at birth and that same infant one minute before birth, no difference between an infant one minute before birth and that infant one minute before that, and so on until the moment of conception. This shows, it is argued, that there is no difference between a newborn infant who has a right to life and a newly fertilized ovum. In other words, the fertilized ovum must have the same right to life that the infant has. Though not perfectly clear, it does seem that C. Everett Koop is arguing something like this when he says, "My question to my pro-abortion friend who will not kill a newborn baby is this: 'Would you kill the infant a minute before he was born, or a minute before that?' You see what I am getting at. At what minute can one consider life to be worthless and the next minute consider that same life to be precious?"[13]

It may be that what is in operation here is what has been called the "fallacy of the continuum," which "is committed when it is argued that because there is a continuous distribution of differences between two extremes, there is no 'real' difference."[14] By this mode of reasoning one could show, for example, that there is no difference between night and day, since as you move from twelve midnight to twelve noon there is never any discernible difference from one moment to the very next. But clearly that is absurd, and this form of reasoning is invalid.

Difficulties with Arguments for a Right to Life from Conception

If it is claimed that from conception onward there exists an individual with the same right to life that we grant to persons,

13. Koop, *The Right to Live, the Right to Die* (Wheaton, Ill.: Tyndale, 1976), p. 27.

14. Alex C. Michalos, *Improving Your Reasoning* (Englewood Cliffs, N.J.: Prentice-Hall, 1970), p. 86.

then we are struck with certain oddities. The first is that the use of the intra-uterine device (IUD) and the so-called morning-after pill, both of which serve to induce abortion,[15] is as serious a moral offense as causing the death (in comparable circumstances) of a seven-month-old fetus, a newborn infant, a child, or an adult. Even if we grant that we ought to have some moral reservations about the use of the IUD and the morning-after pill—reservations that we need not have with respect to contraceptive devices that merely prevent fertilization—it is nevertheless hard for most people to believe that these methods are as morally objectionable as the conservative position would seem to demand. Causing the death of a newly fertilized ovum does not seem as intrinsically objectionable as causing the death of, say, a person sitting next to me.[16] For most people, using the IUD seems more like contraception in its moral seriousness than like infanticide, manslaughter, or possibly even murder, to which the conservative position compares it.

A second point we ought to consider is that approximately one-third of all fertilized ova never implant in the uterine wall,

---

15. "There is some question as to just how the IUD prevents pregnancy but basically it is assumed to do one of two things: either it prevents fertilization from occurring by speeding the egg through the fallopian tubes and uterus and out before fertilization can occur, or its presence in the uterine cavity creates a chemical hostility that prevents implantation of the fertilized egg.... There is also retroactive contraception in the form of a 'morning after' pill that induces actual miniature abortions if fertilization has taken place. This method, which is used for rape victims, causes severe vomiting and nausea and involves large dosages of estrogen which, although potentially harmful, seldom are." R. Bruce Sloane and Diana F. Horvitz, *A General Guide to Abortion* (Chicago: Nelson Hall, 1973), pp. 244, 249.

16. It might be argued that keeping a fertilized ovum from implanting (e.g., by means of the IUD) is not as serious as removing a fertilized ovum that is already implanted (which is what happens in most abortions). But this is not obviously so. In fact, an analogy that readily comes to mind suggests otherwise. Consider the difference between preventing a person from being connected to a life-support system and disconnecting a person who is already connected, both acts causing the patient's death. In essence the two acts would seem to share a common moral status: if the one is a morally unacceptable act, so is the other and equally so. However, even if removing an implanted ovum is more serious than preventing a fertilized ovum from being implanted, still, on the assumption that fertilized ova are persons, the latter act would nonetheless be a grave act, seriously wrong and way out of keeping with what most people would judge to be the actual seriousness attaching to the use of the IUD.

being carried away in the menstrual flow.[17] In other words, these fertilized ova are spontaneously aborted without the woman ever being aware of the fact. But if the conceptus has the value of a person, then these spontaneous abortions ought to be viewed as a natural tragedy of vast and virtually unparalleled proportions, not unlike an unrelenting plague or disease systematically killing one-third of the world's population. Obviously most people would find it difficult to accept such an interpretation. Nevertheless, if the conservative position is correct and zygotes have as strong a right to life as adults, then we who are able should be as morally compelled to use our medical technology to save them as we are morally compelled to save, for example, the large numbers of people perishing from lack of food in parts of Africa today.

A third moral consideration involves the fact that a very high percentage of abnormalities have been discovered in cases of spontaneous abortions; figures range up to 61 percent.[18] At the present time approximately one in every fifty babies is born with some sort of congenital abnormality, mostly of a relatively mild order. But if spontaneous abortion did not occur, the estimate is that this percentage would skyrocket to one in ten or possibly one in five. Most of these defects would be much more severe than those found in the present spectrum of congenital disease and would turn pregnancy and birth into a nightmare. But suppose we discovered a drug that would totally eliminate spontaneous abortions, a drug that produced no bad side-effects and was no more expensive than an aspirin tablet. The argument for a right to life from conception would seem to suggest that people would be morally obliged to take this drug, for if the zygote has a person's claim to life, then it has the right to be protected not only from intentional abortion but also from natural, unintended abortion when reasonable measures are available for doing so. We might grant, even if only for the sake of argument, that taking life is morally worse than not saving life, but that would

---

17. Clinical studies suggest that "one fertilized ovum in three perishes before pregnancy is recognized and one in four or five is lost after the diagnosis of pregnancy has been established. In total ... one fertilized ovum in two is aborted spontaneously" (Malcolm Potts et al., *Abortion* [Cambridge: Cambridge University Press, 1977], p. 60).

18. This datum and what follows can be found in Potts et al., pp. 45-64, along with ample reference to various other technical literature.

not in any way undercut the very strong obligation we have to save life whenever we are in a position to do so. The consequence of saving all these lives would, of course, be horrendous; gross congenital deformity would become commonplace, among other things.

I think it is not unreasonable for individuals to argue that they are more certain that these odd implications are unacceptable than they are that the unqualified right-to-life-from-conception position is true. But even though the moral price that one has to pay in order to accept the right-to-life-from-conception position is clearly high, it still has much to recommend it and remains one of the main options in the abortion debate. While not specifically taught in either the Old or New Testaments, it does not conflict with biblical teachings, and it certainly represents one way—even if not the only way—to capture the high regard for fetal life that is affirmed in Scripture and in the Christian tradition in general. For those of us for whom biblical sanction represents an important consideration, this constitutes no small recommendation for the theory. In addition, there is an admirable consistency and appealing simplicity to this theory. There are no suspicious ad hoc qualifications made to avoid hard cases. And for those who have a strong preference for placing one's moral trust in principles and very little in one's preanalytic intuitions, this is a very attractive theory. But still for many the implications are sufficiently difficult to accept that there seems sufficient warrant to continue to search to find a better way— though I feel impelled to add that it is not easy to find that better way.

DECISIVE MOMENT THEORY TWO: IMPLANTATION

On about the sixth or seventh day following conception, the zygote implants in the uterine wall after having traveled through the uterine tube and circulated in the uterine cavity for a brief period. Following conception the fertilized egg progressively splits into smaller cells so that by the time of implantation there exists a 150-cell organism. But there are two distinguishing features that may prompt people to view implantation as the critical juncture that separates an individual with a person's claim to life from one without it.

First, the implanted conceptus has a firmer hold on life than the free-floating zygote—which is to say that the chances of the zygote developing without interruption to infancy are significantly better from the time of implantation onward. Thus, to use either the IUD (assuming it works by preventing implantation from occurring) or the morning-after pill is to terminate the life of an organism that has a significantly smaller chance of continuing to live than does the implanted conceptus. But is such a consideration relevant in determining whether or not someone possesses a right to life or not? An analogy would seem to suggest that it does not. Should the fact that one individual happens to have only one chance in a hundred of recovering from a potentially fatal illness while another has one chance in two be judged relevant in determining which is a holder of a right to life? I think not. The one life could not be taken with greater impunity simply because the chances of survival were not so good. To kill *either* individual, apart from very unusual circumstances, would be an act of murder, and in both instances a person's claim to life would have been equally denied.

A second significant consideration in support of this theory is that the implanted conceptus is beyond the point where twinning can take place.[19] Twinning is the splitting of the zygote in two, creating identical twins. The implanted conceptus is also beyond the point where the rarer phenomenon of untwinning occurs—that being a combining of a double fertilization (i.e., nonidentical twins) into a single organism with one individual ultimately emerging. It may be judged that before this point we do not have a stable, continuous identity. If we assume that the fetus is a person prior to implantation, then we would also have to accept the notion that one person could become two and two persons could become one. This might lead some people to the claim that we can't have a person until we reach that point where a stable identity exists. But is this convincing? There is reason to doubt that it is.

---

19. This is not quite right, since 4 percent of twinning takes place well after implantation (see R. F. R. Gardner, *Abortion: The Personal Dilemma* [Grand Rapids: William B. Eerdmans, 1972], p. 123). Even without this complication the theory has its problems, but to accommodate this difficulty we might alter the theory to "implantation plus X days," where X specifies that time beyond which twinning does not occur.

Imagine that we lived in a world in which a certain small percentage of teenagers replicated themselves by some mysterious natural means, splitting in two upon reaching their sixteenth birthday. We would not in the least be inclined to conclude that no human being could therefore be considered a person prior to becoming sixteen years of age; nor would we conclude that life could be taken with greater impunity prior to replication than afterward. The real oddity—to press the parallel—would be two teenagers becoming one. However, in all of this we still would not judge that individual's claim to life to be undermined in any way. We might puzzle over questions of personal identity (philosophers' traditional inquiries into such matters would assume a greater practical import), but we would not allow these strange replications and fusions to influence our thinking about an individual's right to life. Nor therefore does it seem that such considerations are relevant to determining the point at which an individual might assume a right to life *in utero*.

DECISIVE MOMENT THEORY THREE:
THE APPEARANCE OF AN EXTERNAL HUMAN FORM

It may be claimed that when a fetus develops a recognizable human form it can be considered an individual with a person's right to life. By external human form I have in mind the development of arms, hands, fingers, legs, feet, toes, genitalia, a face with eyes, nose, mouth, and ears, and so on. Certainly there does come a point at which all of us would be inclined to say that the fetus "looks like a little baby." Where this point comes may to some extent be a matter of subjective judgment, although not altogether. It is difficult to suppose that anyone could look at a fifteen-week-old or even an eleven-week-old fetus and not be prompted to say that it looks like a small baby.

Of course the appeal to human form is emotionally powerful. Pro-life groups use pictures of aborted fetuses most effectively to press home their contention that the fetus has a person's claim to life and that abortion is seriously wrong. Critics often charge that such a use of pictures of dead fetuses, replete with dismembered arms and legs, is sheer sensationalism, but I think there is a greater danger in failing to honestly confront the full character of what is involved in aborting fetal life. Whatever the exact moral implications of the facts, those facts still ought to be confronted. After seeing such pictures, many people gain a new respect for fetal life and conclude that abortion is more morally problematic than they had suspected.

But despite the emotional power and practical value of photographs of developing fetuses, the initial question remains: Does the fact that a fetus has a recognizable human form endow it with a right to life? Or, as Laura Purday and Michael Tooley have put it, "If pig fetuses resembled adult humans, would it be seriously wrong to kill pig fetuses? Or if human fetuses looked like frogs, not adult humans, would abortions be morally permissible? Surely not."[20] Whatever the moral significance we attach to the attainment of human form—and I think it does have significance—it does not constitute personhood, nor does it logically entail the possession of the right to life.

DECISIVE MOMENT THEORY FOUR: THE POINT OF VIABILITY

Viability is reached at that point in the development of the fetus when it can survive outside the womb, independently of its mother's body. Of course, in order to survive at this point it would still have to be fed by someone and cared for in various other ways, and to that extent it remains a dependent organism. If it is born prematurely it may even need considerable medical assistance.

Viability is often chosen by those of a more liberal persuasion on the abortion issue as that point beyond which the fetus has a right to life and before which it does not. At the popular level it has wide support as being the decisive moment from which point on fetal life must be respected. But there are serious problems with this view. For one thing, there seems no reason to believe that an individual either becomes a person or gains a person's right to life by virtue of its being able to continue to live independently of the functioning of the mother's body. It is certainly not a consideration that we would be willing to apply in other contexts, as Jonathan Glover has pointed out:

> Suppose some very old person could be kept alive only at the cost of some physical dependence on another person's body.

---

20. Purday and Tooley, "Is Abortion Murder?" in *Abortion: Pro and Con*, ed. Robert L. Perkins (Cambridge, Mass.: Schenkman, 1974), p. 138.

With improved medical technology, we might be able to plug into other people for periods of the day to make use of the organs we lacked. If an old woman were kept alive only by being dependent on her husband in this way, she would not be "viable." Yet, we would surely continue to count her as a person. Supporters of the theory that viability is the boundary at one end of life have to explain why it is not equally relevant at the other end.[21]

We must not confuse having a right to use another person's body for survival with having a right to life per se. The old woman may not have a right to be plugged into her husband's body, but she certainly has a right to life and does not lose her right to life upon losing her viability. So why should we believe that a fetus lacks a right to life because it is not viable?

Another consideration we ought to take into account is that viability is a relative notion—relative, that is, in terms of advancing modern technology. With talk of constructing artificial wombs, it is conceivable that viability can be pushed back to very early stages of pregnancy, in which case those who support the right of women to have abortions must ask themselves whether they are advocating simply that women have the right to the removal of the fetus from their wombs, or whether they are arguing that the woman has the right to the death of the fetus. Typically the removal of the fetus from the womb of the woman will, during the first six months of pregnancy, result in its death no matter how it is removed. But with improved modern technology, aborting the pregnancy does not automatically kill the fetus: methods are now available to remove the fetus from the womb and to continue to preserve its life artificially. However, in many abortions, the woman desires the death of the fetus, not wanting it to develop into a child that would be hers at all, even if adopted and cared for by others. Surely this is true in the case of most abortions prompted by considerations of genetic deformity. And in many other cases, the woman would very likely go through with the pregnancy if the only alternative were the removal of the fetus, its nurture in an artificial womb, and finally its adoption by others. This suggests that much popular talk of the right to have an abortion is really a euphemistic way of speaking about a right to the death of the fetus. In

---

21. Glover, *Causing Death and Saving Lives* (New York: Penguin Books, 1977), pp. 124–25.

this context, talk of the woman's right to control what happens in and to her body may be terribly misleading, for what the woman really wants is not simply the removal of what is growing in her body (an act of transfer) but the death of the fetus (an act of killing).

DECISIVE MOMENT THEORY FIVE: THE BEGINNING OF BRAIN FUNCTION

At least as early as the eighth week it is possible to record brain waves in the developing fetal brain, and by the twelfth week the structure of the brain is complete. The central importance of the brain in making possible personal existence and sustaining it might suggest that its emergence in the course of fetal development renders the fetus a person. This is a claim that has been extensively argued for and is worthy of careful consideration. The position is basically this: "The scientist measures the definitive end of human life by the end of human brain function as measured by the E.E.G. Why not also then use the onset of that same function as measured on that same instrument as the latest time when a scientist would say that human life begins!"[22]

In his important book on abortion, Baruch Brody contends that the fetus becomes a human being with a right to life at the end of the sixth week, when primitive brain functioning begins.[23] He uses the concept of brain death to determine the essence of humanity—that is, to determine that property which every human being must have in order to be a human being. For Brody the key to identifying this property is determining that which a human being cannot lose without ceasing to exist. So, the argument goes, we can determine that feature the *presence* of which gives one a human being's right to life by determining that property the *absence* of which makes one no longer a human being with a right to life. This procedure seems reasonable enough. So the crucial question becomes, What must happen to a person for that person to cease to exist as an historical being?

Brody argues that only when there has been irreparable brain damage can a human being cease to exist. The flip side of

---

22. Dr. and Mrs. J. C. Wilke, *Handbook on Abortion* (Cincinnati: Hayes, 1975), p. 18.

23. Brody, *Abortion and the Sanctity of Human Life* (Cambridge, Mass.: MIT Press, 1975), p. 109.

this is: any human organism that has *not* suffered an irreparable cessation of brain function (i.e., any human organism that can sustain its own personal life) can be considered a human being with a right to life. An individual in a *reversible* coma who will subsequently regain normal brain functioning would be in this category; so would a six-week-old embryo. Both, according to Brody, have a right to life because both have brains that have a potential for normal functioning. In the case of the fetus, growth and maturation of the brain is required, whereas in the case of the individual in a reversible coma, natural healing of some kind may be required; according to Brody this difference is not morally significant.

But isn't there really a difference between the reversibly comatose individual and the six-week-old embryo? The reversibly comatose possesses a functioning brain that will enable the individual to come out of the coma and to *resume* a personal existence. But that is not what the fetus possesses. Rather, the fetus has a functioning brain that makes possible the prospect of *first-time* personal existence. Surely it could be argued that it is the prospect of a *resumption* of personal consciousness that gives the reversibly comatose a right to life. It is not simply that when the coma lifts—lo and behold—a person will emerge and develop; what we anticipate is the return of the personal being who existed before the coma. It is Mary whom we all knew and loved, who knew and loved us, etc., that will come out of the coma. Or it is Harry, the college student, who wants to become a lawyer but who is now comatose. But none of this applies to the fetus. The prospect for first-time personal life simply is not the same thing as the prospect for continuing personal life. Manifestly, Brody's appeal to the reversibly comatose does not transfer logically to the six-week-old fetus. The fact that one has a right to life does not entail that the other does.

At a more fundamental level, Brody's mistake seems to be that he is attempting to identify the essence of a human being's right to life by isolating that factor the loss of which brings with it a loss of the right to life. But identifying and properly characterizing that factor is crucial. We can say that it is *brain death*—or, as he does, more specifically, *brain death that ends all prospect for personal existence.* But we can be even more specific, characterizing this loss as *brain death that ends all prospect for continued personal existence.* The latter characterization is certainly the more specific, and it has at least one virtue going for it: it helps capture a difference between embryos and the comatose that can be used to account for our conviction that killing a reversibly comatose person is more serious a matter than killing a human embryo—which I think most of us would judge it to be.[24]

DECISIVE MOMENT THEORY SIX: THE ATTAINMENT OF SENTIENCE

It has been argued that a fetus comes to possess a right to life when it becomes sentient (i.e., capable of experiencing sensations). This would mean that somewhere during the second trimester (and at least by the third trimester), when the fetus is capable of experiencing sensations that it finds agreeable or disagreeable, it can be said to have a right to life—but not before. It is argued that prior to sentience there cannot be right to life because prior to sentience there does not exist a creature that can in any way be harmed, that only beings that can be harmed can have rights because by definition rights protect one from certain harms. In other words, rights protect one's interests, and if one cannot feel or experience anything, then one doesn't have interests and thus nothing to be protected by rights. A being can no more have rights without interests, it is argued, than it can have a smile without a mouth.

---

24. Eike-Henner Kluge argues in a fashion similar to that of Brody, contending that a person is someone who is not only (a) perceptually aware, self-aware, and able to reason and form judgments, but may also be (b) "in a state of constitutive potential with respect to these activities, which is to say it has a neurological system structurally similar to a normal adult human being" (*The Practice of Death* [New Haven: Yale University Press, 1975], p. 98). The reason that (b) has to be introduced into the definition of a person is that it is the only way, according to Kluge, to account for our recognition that those in a deep coma or under anesthesia—and who do not, therefore, fulfill condition (a)—are nevertheless still persons. But this means, according to Kluge, that by the fourth month of gestation we have a person and hence most acts of abortion would be murder (p. 93). Kluge does not make a neurophysiological case when he asserts that by the fourth month of gestation we have individuals with brain structures similar to those possessed by adult humans in a coma or under anesthesia. He does imply that the use of electroencephalograms would indicate as much, although he does not provide any relevant data in support of this. However, the same observation is applicable here as when discussing Brody's version of this argument: what the comatose and anesthetized individuals crucially have in common that gives them their recognized strong right to life is not simply the constitutive potential for personal life but rather the constitutive potential for *continued* personal life.

Nevertheless, even if it is granted that a being without interests cannot have a right to life, it does not follow that beings *with* interests do in fact have a right to life. Such beings might conceivably have a right to be protected from suffering unnecessary pain and still not have a right to life. Organisms that can only experience primitive sensations might be said to have a right to be protected from torture without having a right to continue to experience the primitive sensations they naturally experience.

We will take up the more fundamental question of whether sentience is in fact a necessary condition for a right to life in a subsequent chapter, when we consider the so-called "potentiality principle."

DECISIVE MOMENT THEORY SEVEN:
BIRTH

Birth certainly marks an important juncture in the life of an individual. (We do, after all, celebrate birthdays, not conception days!) At birth the individual leaves the mother's womb and enters the world of human society where the process of socialization begins that will yield an individual who is undeniably a person. It might be said that the chief process occurring in the womb is the development of the biological basis for personal existence, whereas the chief process occurring after birth is the social development that before very long results in the acquisition of personal characteristics by the child.

But although it must be granted that birth is an important event in the life of an individual, it does not at all follow from anything that has just been said that birth transforms what is not a person into what is a person or that it transforms a being with no right to life into a being with a right to life. Birth involves a change of location, from inside the mother's womb to outside, but surely personhood and the right to life is not a matter of location. It should be *what* you are, not *where* you are that determines whether you have a right to life. Nor, as we suggested when discussing viability, should that determination rest on whether one is able to survive independent of another's body. It is true that at birth the child is brought into human society, is cared for and interacted with in a way quite different from what was possible when it was in the mother's womb. However, a newborn chimpanzee can be treated in the same fashion—from time to time some are—and that does not invest them with a right to life.

While the newborn infant is on the verge of personhood, it is not yet a person in the strict sense. It will shortly begin to acquire personal characteristics, but at birth its mental and sensory functioning is often below that of many newborn animals (the horse, for example). Birth, then, does not bring about a magical transformation in the life of the growing infant; it does not in itself invest an infant with a right to life.

CONCLUSION

Up to this point in our discussion we have not been able to ascertain when an individual comes to possess a right to life. It might therefore be tempting to conclude, as some have, that the reason for this is that *none* of the stages of human development so far surveyed—from zygote to infant—involves an individual possessing a right to life. I think it would be a mistake to jump to such a conclusion, however; surely it would be difficult for most of us to accept. But this very conclusion has been drawn by some competent moral philosophers, and it is being skillfully articulated, as we shall see in the next chapter. Nonetheless, rather than despairing in our search, we need to examine theories that seek to provide a systematic account of the right to life, theories that will place the abortion issue and the status of the unborn in a larger framework. In other words we need a theory that will determine which of the following have a right to life and what property or set of properties invests them with a right to life or an inviolate status:

> ova and sperm
> fetuses (zygotes, embryos, and fetuses proper)
> infants
> children
> adults
> the reversibly comatose
> the irreversibly comatose
> the massively retarded (i.e., limited to functioning on a *sub*personal level)
> the less severely retarded (i.e., subnormal in intelligence but not subpersonal)

We will examine three theories based, respectively, on what we will be calling the actuality principle, the potentiality principle, and the species principle. Each principle leads to different conclusions about whether those on the above list have a right to life, and the theories based upon them address the issue of the moral status of the fetus in the wider context of the total scope of the right to life.

5

The Actuality
Principle

Unquestionably the most radical theory on the current scene is what I have christened "the actuality principle." It maintains that an individual comes to possess a right to life *only* when personhood has emerged sufficiently so there is a self-consciousness, an ability to envisage a future for oneself, and a capacity to have hopes and aspirations for that future. Potential for all this counts for nothing, it is argued; only what is actualized is relevant to assigning a right to life. The contention is that it makes no sense to attribute a right to someone who does not have the capacity to desire what he or she supposedly has a right to: if an individual is not capable of having a desire to continue to live, for example, then this individual has no right to the continuation of that life. It is for this reason, the argument often proceeds, that animal shelters that painlessly end the lives of cats and dogs violate no right to life because cats and dogs simply are not capable of desiring a future existence for themselves. Neither do these animals have a fear of passing out of existence, of ceasing to be, even though in certain life-threatening circumstances they instinctively "fight for their lives." Crucially, this means that infants, in addition to cats, dogs, and human fetuses, have no right to life because they too cannot desire a future existence for themselves. Of course this is an extreme view, as difficult in the final analysis to accept for those operating outside the Judeo-Christian tradition as it is for those within it. Nevertheless, it is an important and instructive view that takes us to the heart of a number of critical issues in the present debate. In summary the theory looks like this:

Have a right to life:	Do not have a right to life:
children	fetuses
adults	infants
the reversibly comatose	the irreversibly comatose
the less severely retarded	the severely retarded

At the outset several things should be noted about the radical option. First, it is among the best argued positions on the abortion debate. The name most associated with the position is that of Michael Tooley;[1] the comment has been made that his discussion of the whole abortion topic is "the most convincingly argued in the literature."[2] Second, this denial that infants have a right to life is not only being well argued but is receiving a wide hearing. To be sure, advocacy of the actuality principle, along with a tough-minded acceptance of its implications, has been exclusively the work of professional philosophers, but the anthologizing of articles written by proponents of the actuality principle and the fact that it is advocated in college textbooks does mean that serious discussion of the principle is no longer restricted to low-circulation professional journals. Third, the claim that infants lack a right to life undercuts one of the strongest arguments for a conservative position on the abortion issue: (1) infants have a right to life; (2) there is no morally relevant difference between infants and fetuses; therefore, (3) fetuses have a right to life. If infants lack a right to life, then obviously this argument cannot even get off the ground. Fourth, when fully argued, the position may confront some of us with a tension

---

1. Among Tooley's publications are the following: "A Defense of Abortion and Infanticide," in *The Problem of Abortion*, ed. Joel Feinberg (Belmont, Cal.: Wadsworth, 1973), pp. 51–91; "Is Abortion Murder?" (cowritten with Laura Purdy), in *Abortion: Pro and Con*, ed. Robert Perkins (Cambridge, Mass.: Schenkman, 1974), pp. 129–49; and *Abortion and Infanticide* (New York: Oxford University Press, 1983). Other proponents of this position include Mary Ann Warren ("On the Moral and Legal Status of Abortion," in *Today's Moral Problems*, ed. Tom Wasserstrom [New York: Macmillan, 1975], pp. 120–36), Joel Feinberg ("Abortion," in *Matters of Life and Death*, ed. Tom Regan [New York: Random House, 1980], pp. 183–216), and Jonathan Glover (*Causing Death and Saving Lives* [New York: Penguin Books, 1977], pp. 150–69).

2. Glover, p. 127.

between certain conceptual arguments (e.g., that infants can't sensibly be said to have a right to life) and our moral convictions (e.g., that killing infants is seriously and intrinsically wrong). In constructing a moral theory, we may sometimes have to choose between revising our concepts (if we judge that we have the *logical* freedom to do so) or revising our moral judgments (if we have the *moral* freedom to do so). Fifth, the discussion of rights may prompt us to seek alternative accounts of the evil of murder; we might decide that the wrongness of unjustly taking the life of another person (i.e., someone who undeniably is a person) could better be accounted for without any reference to rights being violated. (Such an option may be especially attractive to those in the Judeo-Christian tradition.) If we could fully establish that murder is intrinsically evil (that it is wrong in and of itself) without any reference to a right to life, then it would be of little consequence that infants (or fetuses) lack a right to life. We shall explore this possibility when we turn to a discussion of the potentiality principle in Chapter Six.

INFANTICIDE AND ABORTION

Critically, the actuality principle involves the *denial* that infants have a right to life.[3] But in making this denial, proponents of the argument are not suggesting that killing infants is of no moral consequence; they are only contending that it is not wrong *intrinsically*, that killing an infant does not violate the *infant's* right to life. And why are growing numbers of commentators on the abortion debate even interested in denying that infants have a right to life? In part because they want to establish the acceptability of abortion, and they have done so by arguing that *fetuses* have no right to life; but these arguments are equally effective in showing that newborn infants have no right to life

---

3. We might be tempted to think that infants do not have rights of *any* kind because they cannot invoke rights, protest the abuse of their rights, forego the exercise of a right should they choose, or in general do the sorts of things that persons do with their rights. It might be argued that in order to have a right one must be able to wield that right. But it is more plausible to believe that if there were some sort of proxy who could invoke the rights on behalf of a given individual (whether or not not that proxy actually chose to do so), then that would be sufficient to ensure that the given individual did indeed possess rights—as, for instance, parents and other members of society might invoke rights of behalf of fetuses, infants, and the comatose.

either. Such individuals have simply been tough-minded enough to accept the implications for infanticide inherent in their arguments for abortion.

Peter Singer acknowledges the implications of this sort of argumentation when he states, "I have argued that the life of a fetus is of no greater value than the life of a nonhuman animal at a similar level of rationality, self-consciousness, awareness, capacity to feel, etc., and that since no fetus is a person no fetus has the same claim to life as a person. Now it must be admitted that these arguments apply to the newborn baby as much as to the fetus." He does not disguise his position; with words many will find both blunt and offensive, he proceeds to say, "If the fetus does not have the same claim to life as a person, it appears that the newborn baby does not either, and the life of a newborn baby is of less value than the life of a pig, a dog, or a chimpanzee."[4] The reason he gives for this latter conclusion is that the newborn is at a lower level of rationality, self-consciousness, awareness, capacity to feel, and so forth than is a (grown) pig, dog, or chimpanzee, and Singer denies that the *potential* for rationality and the like (which the infant *does* have) counts for anything at all. Of course, to admit that a potential for personal existence invests one with a strong claim to life would be to give the fetus (as well as the infant) a right to life, and that would render abortion morally problematic.

It turns out, then, that the difficulty with liberal theories on abortion is that they have implications for infanticide that most of us find difficult to accept: the very reasons that deny any special protection to the life of the unborn also serve to deny that special protection to the newly born. Even advocates of the actuality principle are in large part uncomfortable with these implications. Many have sought to reduce the moral embarrassment attaching to their denial that infants have a right to life by arguing that there are still good reasons (other than possessing a right to life) for protecting the lives of infants—reasons that do not in turn call for protecting fetuses (at least not all fetuses). And, of course, it is critical (from their perspective) that the reasons that serve to protect the lives of infants not also apply to fetuses, lest abortion be rendered as unacceptable as infanticide.

---

4. Singer, *Practical Ethics* (New York: Cambridge University Press, 1979), pp. 122-23.

THE EVIL OF INFANTICIDE: ACCOUNTS BY BENN, WARREN, AND ENGELHARDT

S. I. Benn has argued that infanticide ought to be viewed with far more seriousness than abortion despite the fact that infants, like fetuses, lack a right to life.[5] He reasons that acceptance of the practice of infanticide and the attendant attitude that infants are expendable will lead to harsher and less loving treatment of those infants that we do intend to bring to adulthood, which in turn will have effects on the kind of persons that they will eventually become (perhaps leading to emotional impairment or stunting). Benn admits that this has implications for abortion. At the earlier stages of fetal development, when we don't think of the fetus as a "baby in the womb," abortion would have no brutalizing effects on society, he suggests, but at a later stage it might very well have this kind of effect and be, in this regard, very similar to infanticide in its moral gravity. However, it needs to be underscored that, according to Benn, infanticide does not harm the infant who is killed (assuming the killing is done painlessly), nor does it constitute an evil in and of itself. He holds that killing infants is evil only because of the harm it will do indirectly to those other infants who become persons in a society brutalized by the practice of infanticide.

Mary Ann Warren denies that infants have a right to life but maintains that there are good reasons to prohibit acts of infanticide—reasons that do not also serve to prohibit abortion.[6] Her reasoning is that there are people who want infants (if not the parents themselves, then others), and that to destroy the infant is to deny these people the pleasure of having an infant son or daughter. Further, there are people who value infants and wish to keep them alive (even if not for themselves), who are willing to provide the necessary financial support to do so. It would then be wrong, all else being equal, to deny them this opportunity to care for such infants.

Of course, much the same thing can be said of fetuses. They too are valued and wanted, as the enthusiastic commitment of large numbers of people to the Right to Life movement clearly

---

5. See Benn, "Abortion, Infanticide, and Respect for Persons," in *The Problem of Abortion.*
6. See Warren, "On the Moral and Legal Status of Abortion."

demonstrates. Warren acknowledges all this, but maintains that the difference between abortion and infanticide is that denying a woman an abortion means denying her the freedom to determine what happens in and to her own body, perhaps imposing on her considerable hardship, whereas refusing people the opportunity to commit infanticide does not involve denying anyone the freedom to determine what happens in and to her body, nor does it impose grave hardship on anyone (at least in the great majority of cases). Thus, says Warren, "So long as the fetus is unborn, its preservation, contrary to the wishes of the pregnant woman, violates her rights to freedom, happiness, and self-determination. Her rights override the rights of those who would like the fetus preserved."[7]

But if it is the case that killing fetuses can be justified whereas killing infants cannot—and this is so despite the fact that fetuses might be wanted and valued almost as much if not equally as much as infants themselves—then presumably if there came a time when we did not want or value infants, we would be free to go ahead and kill them without moral compunction. Indeed, Warren is willing to accept such a conclusion. She holds that infants ought to be preserved for the same reason that natural resources or great works of art ought to be preserved: because people derive pleasure from them and are willing to support their preservation. But, should conditions alter so that they were no longer wanted and valued, then our obligations would also change—and in this case dissolve completely. Thus, the difference between killing kittens and killing infants is not in the least intrinsic to these acts; it is simply a matter of our getting more pleasure from infants than from kittens—a matter, if you will, of our willingness to spend more for orphanages than for animal shelters. But if our valuations were reversed, then it would be more seriously wrong to kill kittens than infants.

Tristram Engelhardt has argued that with birth the infant assumes a role within society that alters its status and makes infanticide a more serious offense than abortion. He notes that the mother-fetus relationship is automatic and biological, whereas the mother-infant relationship is active and social: "The newborn infant, unlike the fetus, can elicit a series of regular responses and activities from rational humans even though the

---

7. Warren, p. 136.

infant is not itself rational. Even within primitive social contexts, its crying appears as a demand for food, etc., and initiates a series of activities directed to the infant as if it were a person."[8] In contrast, the role of the fetus is *not* social in character, it having no opportunity for the type of interaction that exists between infant and family. Therein lies the seriousness that attaches to infanticide, according to Engelhardt: infanticide involves killing members of the human species who have begun to assume an explicit role within the structure of family and society—this even though infants have yet to achieve full personal life. And what's wrong with killing such individuals? "If nothing else," says Engelhardt, "such destruction would erode the status of the individual within society by undermining the status of a positive active role and relations."[9]

Engelhardt also holds that viability is a critical juncture because from that point on it is possible for the infant to exist outside the womb and thereafter play an active social role. To prohibit abortions from viability onward "has the virtue of preserving social values, such as the dignity and integrity of the role and office of human person."[10] So, ultimately it is not that killing infants or fetal life from viability onward is an intrinsically objectionable activity; rather, it is simply a socially risky activity that might undermine respect for the lives of *other* individuals (ourselves included) who have attained personhood.

THE INTRINSIC EVIL OF INFANTICIDE

In all of the accounts that we have just considered, the evil of infanticide is held to be derivative rather than intrinsic. These same accounts do hold that killing and harming *persons* is intrinsically objectionable, however, and that killing infants is wrong only because it jeopardizes the welfare of these persons by encouraging acts threatening to them. Benn holds that killing infants will hurt the persons who will develop from the infants we don't kill. Warren holds that killing infants will frustrate the desire of people to have and care for those infants. Engelhardt holds that killing infants threatens all persons by undermining the social role of the person. And all three hold that if there were

---

8. Engelhardt, "The Ontology of Abortion," *Ethics* 84 (April 1974), p. 231.
9. Engelhardt, p. 230.
10. Engelhardt, p. 232.

a society in which no such bad consequences flowed from infanticide, then no objection could be raised to the practice. Historically there is reason to believe that just such a society did exist. As W. E. H. Lecky has observed,

> Experience shows that it is possible for men to be perfectly indifferent to one particular section of human life, without this indifference extending to others.... Among the ancient Greeks, the murder or exposition of the children of poor parents was continually practiced with the most absolute callousness, without exercising any appreciable influence upon the respect for adult life.[11]

If infanticide is not intrinsically objectionable, say the proponents of the actuality principle, we must accept the practice with equanimity; if we could transfer the Greek practice into our own culture with no bad side-effects, we should find no moral fault with it. Most of us find such a conclusion impossible to accept, however. Indeed, the denial that there is anything inherently wrong with killing infants has been characterized by one philosopher (Roger Wertheimer), in words that depart from the usual reserve that characterizes philosophical discussions, as an "assault on the conscience and intellect of civilized people" that is "brutal and blundering."[12] The deeply held moral convictions of most people would be in agreement.

The implications of the actuality principle for infanticide not only clash with our common moral consciousness but are also at odds with certain fundamental emphases that characterize the Judeo-Christian tradition. First, there is the doctrine of creation—this being not merely the affirmation that God brought the universe into existence at one time by the free exercise of his power, but also that his creative will continues to be expressed in the ongoing procreative process. The Christian faith holds that the infant is biological human life on the way of becoming personal human life—on the way, that is, to thinking, loving, willing, and worshiping—and that all this is God's intention and purpose for that life. Indeed,

Thou didst form my inward parts,

---

11. Lecky, *History of European Morals* (New York: D. Appleton, 1870), 1: 45.
12. Wertheimer, "Philosophy on Humanity," in *Abortion: New Directions for Policy Studies,* ed. Edward Manier et al. (South Bend, Ind.: University of Notre Dame Press, 1977), p. 35n.15.

thou didst knit me together in my mother's womb....
Thy eyes beheld my unformed substance;
    in thy book were written, every one of them,
the days that were formed for me,
    when as yet there was none of them. (Ps. 139:13, 16)

Further, there is in the Judeo-Christian tradition a profound
sense of gratitude for life as a gift of a loving and gracious God,
a gift that is intrinsically good, whatever the burdens that might
have to be borne to preserve and protect it. Such a gift is not to
be spurned or repudiated but prized and therefore preserved
and protected.

And beyond this, for those who are part of communions
that recognize the sacrament of infant baptism, the low value
that the actuality principle places on infant life will be especially
troublesome. How different is the spirit that animates these
words from the Presbyterian *Book of Common Worship:*

> Dearly beloved, the Sacrament of Baptism is of divine ordinance.
> God our Father, who has redeemed us by the sacrifice of Christ,
> is also the God and Father of our children. They belong with us
> who believe, to the membership of the Church through the cov-
> enant made in Christ, and confirmed to us by God in this Sacra-
> ment, which is a sign and seal of our cleansing, of our engrafting
> into Christ, and of our welcome in the household of God.

According to such a perspective God's grace not only precedes
our response but even precedes our capacity to respond. This is
to acknowledge the profound sense of respect for future possi-
bilities and for latent capacities that characterizes the Christian
tradition. The actuality principle, it would seem, will not readily
find a congenial home in such a tradition. The tradition can, of
course, be qualified or reinterpreted in order to provide that
home, but among the principles we are considering, the actuality
principle requires the most extensive reconstruction of the
Judeo-Christian tradition.

THE ARGUMENT THAT INFANTS HAVE NO RIGHT TO LIFE

The denial that infants have a right to life has typically been
supported by arguments that claim to show that infants lack the
characteristics logically necessary for one to have a right to life,
and although we may feel that only the claim that infants have

a right to life will do justice to our deeply held moral and religious convictions about infant life, still, if the claim itself is not a sensible one, our moral and theological protestations may be in vain. We have to give this matter close consideration.

The denial that infants have a right to life is specifically predicated on the contention that in order for something or someone to have a right of any kind it must have desires and/or interests. It is argued that a stone, for example, cannot intelligibly be said to have a right to be protected from being split in half because a stone has no interest in not being split in half. The reason it makes no sense to attribute rights to that which has no interests, it is argued, is that rights are a protective moral covering for the interests of individuals that they may invoke or that others may invoke on their behalf in order to avoid the sacrifice of those interests—and where there are no interests, there can be no place for a protective moral covering for those interests. It is a conceptual requirement that in order to sensibly say "Jones has a right to X," one must also be able to sensibly say "Having X is in Jones's interest" or "Jones will be harmed if denied X." A right to X, then, is a right to protection from having one's interests violated and being harmed by being deprived of X. So, if we are to successfully contend that infants have a right to life, it is crucial to make sense of the claim that infants are harmed and their interests seriously violated when they are denied the prospect of personal life. This is not the easy task that it at first might appear to be; a good number of moral philosophers have denied it and along with it the claim that infants have a right to life.

We ought to note that in all this talk of rights, no one is equating the rights of an infant with the rights of a stone; that is, no one is suggesting that an infant has no interests or desires in any sense. The argument is not that infants have *no* rights but only that they do not have a right *to life*. Most proponents of the actuality principle would agree that infants have a right to be protected from torture, for example, because torture is clearly contrary to their interests, frustrating as it does a desire (in some sense) to avoid pain. On these grounds, torturing an infant would grossly violate its rights. But the fact that it has *that* right doesn't entail that it also has a right to life or that it has any of a great many other rights (e.g., the right to vote, the right to free speech, the right to have children). In essence, the argument is that individuals are harmed only when their interests are violated and that their interests are violated only when their desires are thwarted. In the case of a right to life, the desire in question is a desire to continue to live, and it is argued that since we know that infants have no such *desire*, it follows that they can have no *interest* in continuing to live and hence that they are not *harmed* when killed, and consequently it follows that talk of infants having a right to life makes no sense.

The reason infants have no desire to continue to live is that they lack the concept of a continuing self, a self that endures through time. An infant has no desire to exist in the future because it does not possess those concepts logically necessary for having such a desire—namely, the concept of time (past, present, future) and the concept of a continuing identical self. Thus, we won't thwart any of an infant's desires if we kill it painlessly. Or, put it this way: to kill a newborn infant painlessly, or to abort a nonviable fetus painlessly, or even to exercise effective birth control measures is in each instance simply to prevent a person from emerging, and this does not harm anyone (i.e., it does not hurt anyone with hopes, aspirations, and desires for the future). To be sure, the individuals who grow to adulthood will be glad that they were not killed in infancy, but then again they will be equally glad that they were not aborted and that their conception was not prevented by contraceptive devices. However, none of these practices—contraception, abortion, and infanticide—harm persons; they simply prevent a person from coming into existence. And the actuality principle specifies that persons do not have a right to come into existence but only a right to continue to exist once they do exist. And as Mary Ann Warren has commented, "The very notion of acting wrongly toward a merely potential person, that is, one which will never become a person, is incoherent. For who is it that is being wronged when a potential person is prevented from becoming a person? Absolutely no one."[13]

To some considerable extent, the valuation of infant life outlined by the actuality principle is a reflection of more crucial attitudes toward fetal life. I think James Humber is correct when he suggests that most advocates of liberal abortion policies adopt that position because they are unable to empathize, sympathize, or identify with a fetus, whereas they are able to empathize,

---

13. Warren, "Do Potential People Have Moral Rights?" *Canadian Journal of Philosophy* 7 (1977): 280.

sympathize, and identify with the suffering and anguish of a pregnant woman.[14] They simply "feel" that abortion is a morally acceptable activity and simply "feel" that the fetus does not have a serious claim to life. Those who defend the actuality principle merely suggest that we go one step further and concede that sympathetic concern for infants is also misplaced. Certainly the infant is cute and cuddly, but so are kittens and puppies. The death of an infant, we are told, harms the infant no more than the death of a zygote harms a zygote. In neither case are hopes, dreams, and aspirations for the future dashed.

CONCLUSION

The actuality principle leads to the conclusion that infants have no right to life, that killing infants is, in and of itself, of no moral consequence. This indicates, I submit, that there is something seriously wrong with this principle. Attempts at reducing the moral embarrassment of the conclusion have not proved successful, nor is it conceivable how they ever could be, seeking as they must to ground the wrongness of infanticide (in one way or another) in its effect on others rather than on the infant. This offends both the biblical tradition and common moral sense. Nevertheless, even if we take issue with the actuality principle, we still have to deal with the argument that it makes no sense to attribute a right to life to infants and fetuses. We will do so as we consider the potentiality principle in the next chapter.

In taking leave of the actuality principle, we might just note that it does have the virtue (if one can call it that) of rendering abortion morally unproblematic. It holds, after all, that neither killing fetuses nor killing infants is intrinsically objectionable, and that one can therefore proceed to have an abortion free from any moral reservations about the nature of the act itself. Indeed, *the only way to have a morally permissive position on abortion is to deny that infants have a right to life,* for as soon as one holds that infanticide is intrinsically objectionable, abortion will inevitably be rendered problematic and morally risky. If I concede that infants possess a right to life and thus an inviolable status, then how can I be sure that fetuses, which are not so very different

---

14. See Humber, "Abortion: The Avoidable Moral Dilemma," *Journal of Value Inquiry* 9 (Winter 1975): 282–302.

from infants, don't also have a right to life? If I want to have this assurance, then I must look for features that I can *with confidence* point to and say "This feature gives all beings who possess it a right to life, and it is possessed by infants but not by fetuses." That is not an easy assignment to fulfill. Until it is fulfilled, I don't see how anyone can with an easy conscience proceed to endorse abortion. The actuality principle at least serves to focus our attention on the fact that the moral status of the *newborn* is crucial to the abortion debate.

6
The Potentiality Principle

Proponents of the potentiality principle hold that a right to life belongs not only to persons but to all who in the course of the normal unfolding of their intrinsic potential will become persons. They assume that a human organism has a "natural" potential for personhood (and here we introduce a technical definition) if it is possible for it to develop into a person without the necessity of outside intervention to invest it with new latent properties, the unfolding of which (when coupled with socialization) will yield a person. According to this view, the *unfertilized* ovum does not have a natural potential for personhood, since it requires the intervention of the male sperm to give it new features which then—and only then—put it on a path that will (with some likelihood) lead to the formation of a person. The fertilized ovum, of course, needs outside *nurture*, but this is required to sustain the organism in its growth rather than to invest it with a growth principle it does not already possess.

The potentiality principle includes fetuses and infants as holders of a right to life but excludes (as does the actuality principle) the severely retarded and irreversibly comatose on the grounds that they have no natural potential for self-reflective intelligence or the exercise of moral self-determination. The overview of the potentiality principle, then, looks like this:

93

Have a right to life:	Do not have a right to life:
fetuses	the irreversibly comatose
infants	the severely retarded
children	
adults	
the reversibly comatose	
the less severely retarded	

In laying stress on the respect due individuals (fetuses and infants) who have a natural potential for rational agency but have yet to actualize that potential, the potentiality principle succeeds in capturing a moral perspective that is also embedded in a number of Judeo-Christian theological themes. The same theological considerations that make it difficult to assimilate the actuality principle into the Judeo-Christian tradition serve to provide a measure of theological support for the potentiality principle. Certainly the potentiality principle preserves the profound sense of respect for latent rational, moral, and spiritual capacities that is evident in such Judeo-Christian theological themes as the concept of life as a gift and therefore a trust from God, the presumption that God as ongoing creator has a divine intent for developing biological human life (namely, that it become personal human life), and the tradition of receiving infants into the household of faith (by means of circumcision and baptism).

Nevertheless, theological tradition cannot by itself transform incoherence into coherence; defenders of the potentiality principle must still come to terms with the contention that a right to life cannot be sensibly attributed to potential persons—to infants and fetuses. This denial hinges, as we have noted in the discussion of the actuality principle, upon the crucial contention that infants do not have an interest in continuing to live, or in other words that painlessly killing an infant does not harm the infant. If rights serve only to protect interests, say the proponents of the actuality principle, and if an infant can't sensibly be said to have an interest in continuing to live, then the infant can't sensibly be said to have a right to life either.

There are several ways to respond to this challenge. First, one can meet it on its own terms, arguing that it does make sense to attribute a right to life to infants because, contrary to what defenders of the actuality principle contend, killing infants does harm infants. Second, it can be argued that not all rights need be understood as protecting against harm and that one can sensibly attribute a right to life to fetuses without having to prove that killing harms. Finally, one can argue that the intrinsic wrongness of killing innocent human beings (including infants) can be fully captured without any reference to the language of rights. Indeed, if this can be done, then it doesn't matter whether or not we can sensibly attribute a right to life to infants. Let us look at these three lines of response in turn.

RESPONSE ONE: AFFIRMING AN INFANT RIGHT TO LIFE

To meet the challenge head on, we need to argue that killing infants harms infants, that it violates their interests in some way or other and therefore makes them suitable candidates for a right to life. This can be done in at least three ways. First, it can be argued that all sentient creatures have interests because all sentient creatures (by definition) have experiences that they find pleasurable or painful. Clearly pleasurable experiences are (all else being equal) in one's interest, and painful experiences are (all else being equal) against one's interest. To be sentient an organism must have feelings or sensations, but it need not have a thought life. To have pleasurable or painful sensations, an organism need not have a concept of the self, a concept of pain or pleasure, a concept of time, or any concepts at all: it need only be able to feel. But if it is not necessary that an organism be able to conceptualize pleasure and pain before its interests can be affected by pleasure and pain, then why should we suppose that an organism must be able to conceptualize such things as life and death before death can be said to affect its interests (as defenders of the actuality principle maintain)?

It would seem that one can harm individuals by denying them a good as well as by inflicting an evil upon them. If that is the case, then killing is one way to harm individuals, since it denies them certain positive sensations by taking from them the possibility of having *any* sensations at all. However, it would follow from this line of argument that *only* those fetuses who are sentient have a right to life and consequently that during the first four to five months of fetal development, when there is no sentience, there would be no right to life. This would be incompatible with the form of the potentiality principle that we have been discussing and that I am interested in defending, since it also attributes a right to life to the fetus prior to sentience, during those first few months of development when this feature is not yet present.

Second, it can be argued that harm can be inflicted on infants by destroying their existence as self-maintaining organisms.[1] Although infants do need nurture and cannot survive on their own, they are at least living biological organisms that function in such a way as to contribute to the maintenance of their own existence. Infants seek to avoid painful stimuli, and thereby they often avoid what would be harmful; they will also feed when hungry, thereby unconsciously contributing to their own survival. To kill an infant, then, is to thwart its thrust for self-maintenance. And since the term *harm* is suitable in this context, it can be argued that the notion of having interests is suitable as well, since it is in an organism's interest to be kept from harm. Moreover, even newly fertilized ova are self-maintaining organisms. Indeed, few if any living organisms, whether sentient or nonsentient, are not. Plants, for example, are self-maintaining organisms: they need water and various nutrients to survive, of course, but they function in their environment in such a way as to contribute to the continuance of that functioning. To be sure, neither plant nor fetus "takes an interest" in continuing to maintain its functioning, but despite this both can be harmed by having this functioning disrupted. (We ask, for example, "Will it *harm* this plant to 'water' it with coffee?''), and so it can be coherently claimed that *a right to life is possessed by all self-maintaining organisms that have a natural potential for personhood.* This last qualification excludes plants and other self-maintaining organisms that have no natural potential for personhood but would include both infants and all fetal life.

There is a third line of argumentation available—namely, that killing infants harms them by depriving them of the prospect of personal existence, a harm that exceeds what could be inflicted on animals, who lack any such prospect. Indeed, if I can harm the sleeping baby by killing it, thereby depriving it of certain physical goods it would have enjoyed upon waking (e.g., stroking, feeding, mothering), then presumably I can harm an infant by depriving it of the personal existence it would have

---

1. For an example of this line of argument, see Philip Devine, *The Ethics of Homicide* (Ithaca, N.Y.: Cornell University Press, 1979), pp. 20–21.

enjoyed upon maturing. The difficulty with this argument, however, is that it involves the problematic presupposition that the infant and the person it develops into are one and the same individual. It obviously makes no sense to argue that an infant can be deprived of personal life unless the individual who is now the infant without personal life is identical with the individual who subsequently acquires personal life. And just as obviously, this is not a problem-free identification. It might be argued, for example, that as a person I am by definition simply a center of self-conscious awareness and therefore that I didn't come into existence until I came into existence as a center of self-consciousness—just as it might be argued that I would cease to exist should I become permanently unconscious and pass out of existence as a center of self-consciousness. Proponents of such a view (and those who deny that infants have a right to life seem to believe something very much like this) would maintain that to have killed the infant from which I in fact ultimately emerged would not have been to kill me, because I am not that infant. They would hold, then, that infanticide, like abortion and contraception, could have prevented me from coming into existence, but it could not have prevented me, as an already existing being, from continuing to exist, because I didn't exist until a personal center of consciousness emerged.

This kind of argument raises difficult and complex problems about personal identity and the nature of the self, problems that continue to bedevil philosophers. But some remarks may help. We should note, for example, that this kind of argument identifies the self with self-consciousness, and such a view of the self dictates not only that I don't come into existence until I emerge as a self-conscious being, but that I don't exist when asleep or in a coma, since under such circumstances I am not conscious at all, let alone self-conscious. Clearly this is a curious conclusion. Common sense tells me that I continue to exist even though I am not conscious. Hence the objection: If I can exist though not conscious, then why can't I exist though not yet self-conscious? Indeed, newborn infants are conscious; it is simply that their consciousness is not reflexive (i.e., they are not yet self-aware). We might very well suppose that if a given individual can at one time be unconscious (because comatose) and at another time self-conscious (having come out of the coma), then a given individual (as an infant) can be conscious and later *self*-conscious (as a young child). From this it would follow that the infant can be deprived of self-consciousness by being killed.

When I say that the infant can be *deprived* of self-consciousness and therefore harmed I am not saying that it can be subjected to a *conscious* loss but simply that it can be denied the acquisition of certain very valuable features or characteristics that it would naturally and in due course have come to possess. I think it quite fair to say that one need not be aware of having suffered the loss, harm, or deprivation to have actually suffered them: it simply isn't true that what you don't know won't hurt you. If I were cheated out of a just inheritance that I didn't know I had, I would be harmed regardless of whether I knew about the chicanery. Deprivation of a good (be it an inheritance or self-conscious existence) constitutes harm even if one is ignorant of that deprivation. Killing infants harms them even though they are ignorant of the harm that befalls them.

RESPONSE TWO: AFFIRMING A MODIFIED INFANT RIGHT TO LIFE

It is possible to look at rights (or at least some rights, including the right to life) in a slightly different way than has been suggested up to this point. We need not understand all rights as protecting against *harm;* we can also understand them as protecting against violations of individual *autonomy.* In other words, we might conceive of some rights as defining specified spheres in which we judge the individual to be sovereign—that is, areas in which the *individual* is entitled to exercise control, for better or worse, free from interference by others. Consider, for example, the right to religious liberty, which entitles us to make those decisions that define us as religious beings and which also entitles us to practice our religion as we see fit—contingent, of course, upon respect for the rights of others. We hold that this right prevails even in cases in which we judge a given religious adherent to be in serious error. Thus, the right to religious liberty does not presuppose possesssion of the truth. Nor is it grounded in the Greatest Happiness Principle. People may in fact be *happier* possessing religious autonomy, but this is not the reason we support a right to religious liberty. Indeed, if we were to determine that people would be happier if we made their religious decisions for them (by means of sophisticated brainwashing techniques, say), that would not make it right to do so. It would be a violation of their right to religious liberty should we succeed.

In a similar fashion we can argue that the right to life protects individual sovereignty over one's own existence, that to kill the innocent would constitute a usurpation of personal autonomy and therefore be a violation of individual rights, regardless of whether such individuals could (in some sense) be said to be "better off dead." So even if it were the case that we would not harm them by killing them, we would nevertheless violate their right to life by preempting a decision-making authority that is rightfully theirs, not ours. To respect an individual's right to life, then, is to respect the right of the individual to determine whether he or she will continue to exist. Of course, it would follow from such an account that if I were to kill an individual with that individual's consent, I would not have violated a right to life because I would not have violated anyone's autonomy. Would such an act be morally permissible then? Not necessarily. Killing can be wrong for reasons other than that it violates a right to life. It may actually harm the individual, though he or she through misjudgment fails to see this. It may violate God's sovereignty over life. It may have negative social repercussions. It may be an unjustified sacrifice of a personal center of value. So waiving one's right to life does not give others carte blanche to kill. It merely follows that it is not wrong for *that* reason.

But can we violate a fetus's or an infant's autonomy by killing it? That is, can we violate the autonomy of beings who are not yet moral agents (as fetuses and infants are not) by terminating their lives and thereby preventing moral agency from ever even emerging? There would be no agency or autonomy present to violate; we would not be acting contrary to the actual wishes, wants, and desires of the infant or the fetus. But to declare that infants *do* have a right to life would be a way of declaring that *human sovereignty over developing human life belongs to the moral agent who will ultimately emerge from that developing human life*. And this does not seem an odd claim at all. After all, we would not kill a person who was in a lengthy coma because she had temporarily (for a year or so) lost her capacity for moral agency. Of course it could be argued that to kill such a person would be to violate the autonomy of the precomatose moral agent who, prior to falling into the coma, wanted to live. In this regard the fetus/infant case is different from the comatose patient case, for neither fetuses nor infants have a prior wish to live.

To change the case slightly, let us now imagine an individual who wished to *die* prior to entering a coma but who we have reason to believe will wish to *live* after coming out of the coma. Suppose that empirical studies have established that ninety percent of all those entering a coma wanting to die will come out of the coma wanting to live. That being the case, killing comatose individuals would certainly violate their personal autonomy and their right to life—not because it would entail a violation of *past* wishes or desires (since prior to falling into the coma the individual actually wanted to die) but because there would be a violation of future wishes or desires (since we know that the individual will wish to live after coming out of the coma). Indeed, in this case the act of killing violates the autonomy of the agent who will be functioning *after* the coma is over—a situation similar to that of the fetus or infant. To kill a fetus or an infant is contrary to the almost universal desires of those agents who will naturally and in due course develop from them, for they invariably wish to live. And when do future wishes and wants have to be taken into account? Those who opt for an infant right to life answer: Whenever there is a natural potential for developing into a being with such wishes. Therefore, in acknowledging the right to life of a fetus or the right to life of an infant, we are declaring that whether or not the life that has begun is allowed to continue is solely up to the agent who will subsequently emerge. Surely that is an intelligible claim.

RESPONSE THREE: AFFIRMING THE INTRINSIC WRONGNESS OF KILLING INFANTS

Despite what we have said thus far, it remains the case that not everyone will be convinced that infants and fetuses have a right to life. Indeed, some people find the whole notion of moral rights to be conceptually problematic. They agree with Jeremy Bentham's conclusion that "Natural rights is simple nonsense: natural and imprescriptible rights, rhetorical nonsense—nonsense upon stilts." Many operating within the Judeo-Christian tradition are also unreceptive to the notion that what makes killing wrong is the fact that persons have a right to life, because they contend that such an emphasis overlooks God as an important feature of the moral situation. It is not that killing me violates my right to life, they argue, so much as it violates God's sovereignty over life and his authority to determine the circumstances under which life is to be taken. In this spirit, Dietrich Bonhoeffer (in remarks referring to abortion but certainly applicable to infanticide) has commented, "The simple fact is that God certainly intended to create a human being, and this nascent human being has been deliberately deprived of his life."[2] Infanticide is wrong because it contravenes a divine intention for the infant's life, not because it contravenes the infant's right to life. Indeed, the Old and New Testaments emphatically condemn the killing of the innocent without ever introducing (at least explicitly) the notion of a violation of a right to life. Likewise, Greek ethics operated without the concept of a right to life (at least not explicitly—and it is by no means clear that it was even implicitly present). The notion of possessing any kind of right was not explicitly introduced into moral discourse until William of Ockham did so in the fourteenth century. As Kurt Baier has suggested,

> The language of rights is not essential to moral language. It does not figure in ancient or medieval ethics. Questions it would now be perfectly natural to formulate in terms of rights—for example, whether a starving man has a right to steal food from someone who has plenty—would have been asked in terms of whether it was right, lawful, just, licit, or permissible for him to do so.[3]

The challenge presented by advocates of the actuality principle—namely, that an infant right to life makes no sense—might be met obliquely rather than head on. By abandoning all talk of a right to life, we might formulate our rejection and condemnation of infanticide solely in terms of what is unlawful, impermissible, and wrong. This would enable one to avoid the tangled discussion that centers on the question of whether it makes sense to attribute a right to life to infants (my earlier comments represent only the beginning of such a discussion) and proceed to suggest that the life of an infant ought to be respected because from the infant will emerge a self-determining agent, capable of moral and spiritual response. This would be to endorse the moral principle that *it is wrong to kill what will naturally and in due course develop into a person*. This principle makes no reference to a right

---

2. Bonhoeffer, *Ethics* (New York: Macmillan, 1955), p. 176.

3. Baier, "When Does the Right to Life Begin?" in *Human Rights*, ed. J. Roland Pennock and John W. Chapman (New York: New York University Press, 1981), p. 202.

to life but nevertheless provides a basis on which to condemn acts of infanticide as intrinsically objectionable and to place on all moral agents the duty to refrain from such acts. Lying behind this principle is the more general principle that, in Alan Donagan's words, "If respect is owed to beings because they are in a certain state, it is owed to whatever, by its very nature, develops into that state."[4] Both of these principles can be accepted and understood without any reference to a right to life.

We might give an account of the wrongness of killing not only potential persons but actual *persons* as well in terms that omit any reference to a violation of a right to life. It can be argued that the life of a person ought to be respected and held inviolable on the grounds that for rational self-determining agents, existence is the divinely appointed occasion to seek God (see Acts 17:26-27) and in general to determine ultimate loyalties and live them out—to participate, in other words, in a process that has as its outcome one's destiny as a moral and spiritual being. Indeed, as Karl Barth maintained, life is "the one great opportunity of meeting God and rejoicing in his praise."[5] And since to kill a person is to frustrate that opportunity, it can be argued that killing is wrong for much the same reason that it is wrong to use force or nonrational manipulative means to impose a value system on people that is not of their own choosing: it prevents the realization of the divine intention for that life, the living out of freely chosen life purposes. Of course killing is even more seriously wrong because it constitutes the ultimate invasion into the life of another; it involves a permanent end of all temporal opportunity to live out life purposes and thus participate in a process initiated by God himself. The case could be made that to respect the lives of persons is to respect the divine calling that each person has (for each individual is a participant in a drama, the outcome of which is his or her moral and spiritual destiny), and it is wrong to kill innocent persons because it is an unjust interruption of the divinely conferred occasion to pursue life purposes.

In contemporary discussion, those who abandon talk of a right to life are usually understood to be embracing a utilitarian

---

4. Donagan, *The Theory of Morality* (Chicago: University of Chicago Press, 1977), p. 171.

5. Barth, *The Doctrine of Creation*, vol. 3 of *Church Dogmatics* (Edinburgh: T. & T. Clark, 1961), p. 336. Cf. Acts 17:26-27.

account of the wrongness of killing. I want to stress that this is not the case with the argument we have just considered. Indeed, it is because they reject utilitarian accounts of the wrongness of killing that many professional commentators explicitly appeal to the "right to life" and in general use "rights" language. Such critics are concerned that utilitarians too readily allow individual rights to be infringed upon in order to secure certain social gains. In some circumstances violating rights may actually maximize overall happiness as the principle of utility requires. The life that is to be protected today because its *preservation* furthers the common good may be a candidate for destruction tomorrow because its sacrifice will further the common good. Wary of such dangers, "rights theorists" affirm, to the contrary, that rights are morally basic, that there are certain fundamental rights—including the right to life—that ought not to be sacrificed for the sake of increasing the overall amount of happiness in the world.

In this debate between utilitarians and rights theorists, most Christians identify with the latter—and I think correctly so. The respect owed individuals with full moral standing is, from the Christian point of view, grounded not in the temporal interests of human society but in the absolute claim of God. It is God who has called the individual into existence for his own purposes and ends, and those purposes ought not to be set aside in the name of the collective interest of society. But the argument based on the principle that it is wrong to kill what will naturally and in due course develop into a person avoids any utilitarian implications even though it departs from rights language.

THE SEVERELY RETARDED AND THE OVERFLOW PRINCIPLE

Before proceeding in our discussion, we should take note of one difficulty implicit in *all* versions of the potentiality principle. Just as the actuality principle leads to the embarrassing conclusion that infants have no right to life, so the potentiality principle leads to the conclusion that the severely retarded have no right to life on the grounds that they have no potential for personhood (or, setting aside the concept of a right to life, we can say that it leads to the conclusion that killing the severely retarded is not intrinsically objectionable). Obviously most people would consider such a conclusion to be morally awkward. I think it safe to say that there is a common assumption that the lives of such

individuals ought not to be simply tossed aside. They too are
God's creatures and worthy of respect.

However, it is not beyond *all* doubt that the life of a severely
retarded individual ought to be inviolable in the way that we
feel the life of a person or potential person ought to be inviolable,
granting that the individual is *completely and forever* incapable of
functioning above a brute level. (I want to make it very clear that
I am thinking of the extreme cases of retardation, about individuals who are unable to function above an animal level. I am *not*
talking about less severely retarded inviduals, such as partici-
pants in the Special Olympics, for whom personal existence is
present, though stunted.) To be sure, there may be some other
very good reasons for not killing the grossly retarded. Surely
there would be considerable danger involved in drawing lines
("Here rationality is adequately developed, but there it is not"),
and there is a strong possibility that if we as a society were to
kill the severely retarded as a matter of course, the practice
would blunt our sensitivity and respect for other human life, and
of course there would be an ongoing danger of mistaken diagnosis and prognosis. Still, the denial that the life of the severely
or massively retarded is inviolable is not easy to accept, even
after these practical reasons for respecting their lives have been
acknowledged. I think most people instinctively feel on the one
hand that it would be more seriously wrong to kill an adult
person or a normal newborn than it would be to kill a grossly
retarded individual, and on the other hand that it would be a
much more serious act to kill a severely retarded human than to
kill a dog or cat.

A comment by Philip Devine may help to resolve some of
this difficulty, serving to reduce the moral tension that sympa-
thizers with the potentiality principle may feel. "The principle of
respect for persons," he says, "also extends by what might be
called the overflow principle, to things closely associated with
persons. Thus corpses ought not to be treated as ordinary garbage, and one might also argue that a modicum of reverence
should be accorded the process by which persons come to be."[6]

The overflow principle might also be invoked to explain the
respect we feel to be appropriate to the severely retarded. We
don't treat human corpses as garbage, because the corpse is

---

6. Devine, p. 101.

closely associated with persons: it is the remains of a physical organism that at one time supported and made possible personal life. In the case of the severely retarded, the "close association" consists in the fact that such individuals are the kind of living biological organisms through which personal life *normally* manifests itself, though in their particular case it does not and will not. We can say that by virtue of this association they ought to be given a certain respect, while also maintaining that because the association is "an overflow," the respect can be less than what we would give a person (or potential person) and more than we would give a mere animal. By putting the severely retarded in this unique category, a category in which a good measure of special respect is due, we achieve several things. Most importantly, we take the sting out of any denial that the severely retarded have a person's right to life (for we are not thereby reducing them to mere animal status), and we preserve the insight that personhood, with its attendant moral and spiritual capacities (or potential for this), renders each human life valuable and inviolable in a special way.

The overflow principle can also be articulated in terms of a Christian anthropology that views human beings as compound creatures, consisting of (1) self-creative moral and spiritual agency, and (2) the sort of biological functioning that (normally) makes such agency possible. It can be argued that the respect due such compound creatures is a product of both their nature and the fact that they are a divine creation. In the case of a severely retarded individual, however, there is no capacity for agency, because in effect the human biological organism is critically defective. Nevertheless its defects do not render such an organism any less a divine creation, and since it shares the biological form ordained by God to bear moral and spiritual agency, it deserves more respect than is appropriate for mere animals. We may judge that such an individual is *not* in the image of God and that it does not have a person's or a potential person's right to life, but for all that we do not relegate it to the status of an animal (even if we have a high view of animals).

THE BEGINNING OF THE RIGHT TO LIFE

But when does the right to life begin? Or, when does terminating fetal life begin to acquire an intrinsically objectionable character? I think the doctrine of creation favors conception as the correct answer. By "the doctrine of creation" I am referring, more specifically, to the divine intention for developing biological human life. To recognize God as Creator is to identify him with the process by which human beings come into existence, and such an identification is incompatible with a divine indifference toward the fate of either the born or unborn. It seems clear that the One who shapes the process must intend the eventual outcome, which is a personal being, a fully developed human. Further, if we grant that God intends that infant life be preserved and if we agree that killing infants is intrinsically objectionable, then what reason can we give for asserting that this is not also true of fetal life? And in the *absence* of good arguments for discriminating between prenatal and postnatal life and among stages of intra-uterine development, the divine intention should be understood to embrace the fetus at all stages of development from the moment of conception onward. In other words, we would need good reasons before we would be justified in limiting our understanding of the scope of the divine intention. Of course this also means that we ought to be ready to qualify our understanding of the divine intention should those "good reasons" be forthcoming.

To add a useful distinction to our discussion, we might note that the divine intention can be understood in two different ways. First, it can be understood as embracing individuals. We typically think of it in this way with regard to infants, believing that the divine intention for each individual infant (with a potential for personal existence) is that this potential be actualized. In this case the divine intention is, as I shall term it, "individual-specific," and so killing infants would have to be viewed as a contravention of that intention and therefore wrong. But the divine intention can be understood in a second way. It is reasonable to suppose that the divine intention for human sexual intercourse is the production of human persons. In the extent to which the divine will embraces a human activity, it can be considered a "general intention" rather than an individual-specific intention. Surely most people would agree that it is not God's will that each ovum be fertilized and develop into a person or that each act of sexual intercourse result in conception, but rather that human sexual intercourse *generally* succeed in producing human beings. If this is so, then *selective* contraception and *selective* celibacy would not contravene this general intention (human beings would still be produced) whereas *universal* contraception and *universal* celibacy would contravene the divine intention (human beings would no longer be produced). If we grant this distinction, we will have clarified the status of the unfertilized ovum and the infant, but we will remain in the dark about the more problematic status of the fetus:

$$
\begin{aligned}
\text{unfertilized ova} &\rightarrow \text{general divine intention} \\
\text{fetuses} &\rightarrow ? \\
\text{infants} &\rightarrow \text{individual-specific divine intention}
\end{aligned}
$$

Now if we are convinced that the divine intention for each infant life (or at least for each infant life with a potential for personal existence) is that it be preserved and protected, then we seem to be committed to the *same* understanding of the divine intention for fetal life—unless we can provide good reasons for restricting its scope. For if we deny that fetuses are embraced within an individual-specific divine intention and thus deny that they share the same moral status as infants, then there must be significant differences between these two classes of individuals to justify our separate classification. If these difference are not set forth, discriminatory treatment will be arbitrary and morally unjustified. So the critical question is whether there are good reasons for discriminating between infants and fetuses, for believing that the divine intention for the born and the unborn is not the same—for believing, in other words, that infanticide is horrible but abortion is not.

The conservative on the abortion issue denies that there are any good reasons for discriminating between infants and fetuses, insisting that the divine intention for both is individual-specific and that abortion is therefore as objectionable as infanticide. In contrast, the liberal on the abortion issue disagrees, in essence placing the human fetus in the same category with the unfertilized ovum and construing the divine purpose for pregnancy in the same terms as that of sexual intercourse—namely, holding that it is God's will that sexual intercourse and pregnancy succeed in producing persons only *in general*. On the basis of that assumption, the liberal maintains that selective abortion no more contravenes the divine intention than does selective contraception or selective celibacy. In addition to these two alternatives there are more radical options as well, as indicated in Table A.

The problems confronting both the conservative and the liberal positions are similar. The liberal who wants to reject

Table A

	Radical Conservative	Conservative	Liberal	Radical Liberal
unfertilized ovum	individual-specific divine intention	general divine intention	general divine intention	general divine intention
contraception	seriously wrong	permissible	permissible	permissible
fetus	individual-specific divine intention	individual-specific divine intention	general divine intention	general divine intention
abortion	seriously wrong	seriously wrong	permissible	permissible
infant	individual-specific divine intention	individual-specific divine intention	individual-specific divine intention	general divine intention
infanticide	seriously wrong	seriously wrong	seriously wrong	permissible

infanticide but accept abortion has to show why the divine intention changes at birth, ceasing to be general and suddenly becoming individual-specific, for if this is not the case, then it follows that infanticide is no more objectionable than abortion or contraception (the radical liberal position). The conservative, on the other hand, has to show why it is reasonable to believe that the divine intention for newly fertilized ova is individual-specific if it is not individual-specific for *unfertilized* ova or else be saddled with the awkward implication that contraception is as seriously wrong as abortion or infanticide (the radical conservative position). Both the conservative and the liberal, then, are in danger of sliding into moral absurdity. At what point, then, is it reasonable to suppose that the divine intention becomes individual-specific and individual acts of killing become objectionable? Let us review the principal options available to us.

1. Birth

Birth involves a change of location from inside to outside the mother's womb and the termination of an intimate physical connection between mother and fetus, but neither of these changes alters the nature of the fetus itself. There seems to be little warrant for attempting to establish a serious claim to the presence of an individual-specific divine intention for a given life on the basis of its spatial location or the manner in which it receives nourishment and oxygen. Since no significant property attaches to the newborn that does not also characterize the mature fetus, the suggestion that the divine intention becomes individual-specific only at birth has little to recommend it.

2. Viability

There seems no reason to to suppose that God wants individual life preserved only when that life is not dependent upon a woman's womb for its preservation, that he is indifferent to it if it is dependent in that way. To endorse such a view is to say that when life is most vulnerable and in most need of human care, then *God* does not care.

3. Sentience

A case for the attainment of sentience[7] as the beginning point of an individual-specific divine intention could be made if the following argument could be defended: (a) Only sentient creatures have a right to life; (b) only those with a right to life are the objects of an individual-specific divine intention; and therefore (c) only when the human fetus becomes sentient is there an individual-specific divine intention. However, as has been argued earlier, we do not need to link the divine intention that individual life be preserved to a right to life. The divine intention may simply be that what naturally and in due course will develop into a person be held inviolable, and consequently

---

7. L. W. Sumner provides the most thorough defense of the claim that sentience is a necessary and sufficient condition for possessing a right to life, doing so within the context of a utilitarian moral theory. See his book *Abortion and Moral Theory* (Princeton: Princeton University Press, 1981).

preserved and protected. There is no reason to believe that God is impressed only by a right to life. But additionally, reasons have been given in support of the claim that asserting a right to life on behalf of pre-sentient fetuses *does* make sense.

4. Human Form

There would seem to be very little reason to suspect that an individual-specific divine intention commences with the fetus's acquisition of a recognizable human form—arms, hands, fingers, legs, feet, toes, genitalia, a face with eyes, nose, mouth, and so forth. Paraphrasing an earlier quotation from Tooley and Purdy, we might well ask "If pig fetuses looked like adult humans, would it be a contravention of the divine intention to kill pig fetuses? Or if human fetuses happened to look like frogs, not adult humans, would abortion then be consistent with the divine intention? Surely not."

5. Brain Function

The argument that an individual-specific divine intention for a fetus is tied to the emergence of primitive brain functioning does not have any morally awkward implications. But the question remains what positive reasons we can give for believing that a divine intention that the latent properties inherent in the organism unfold and come to fulfillment should come into effect only six weeks after conception and not before. The potential inherent in the organism clearly exists prior to the generation of brain waves, so why should we not assume that the divine intention for that potential also exists prior to the generation of these brain waves?

6. Implantation

Implantation brings with it a firmer hold on life than the free-floating zygote possesses, its chances of surviving being significantly higher. But it would be dangerous to generalize such a consideration; it would lead us to the conclusion that God does not will the preservation or protection of individual human life whenever the chances of survival are minimal.

7. Conception

Decisive arguments are hard to come by in the abortion debate, and we should not expect to find one here. Nevertheless, I believe a reasonable case can be made for conception as the critical juncture at which the divine intention ceases to be general in character and becomes individual-specific. At least I would suggest that conception is a more reasonable proposal than the alternatives we have just considered if only on the basis of a couple of elementary biological facts: first, each human ejaculation contains approximately 200 million spermatozoa, and second, from the 100,000 to 1,000,000 oocytes in a female there will be produced a lifetime maximum of 390 ova.[8] Surely it is too much to believe that the divine intention for each ovum is that it be fertilized (every woman bearing almost 400 children in a lifetime!) let alone that each sperm succeed in fertilizing an ovum (there are just too many spermatozoa per ovum).

If we assume that natural processes, at least in their fundamental outline, correspond to the intention of the Creator, then it is reasonable to believe that the existence of spermatozoa and ova in such superabundance is part of a process that randomly insures that some *but not all* ova will be fertilized, with the greater portion of both ova and sperm simply perishing. It would seem that we are committed to saying that the divine intention for human sexual intercourse is a general one, that only in general is it intended that human beings be conceived by this process. This is a significant conclusion to reach, for it means that we need not grant a special status to the unfertilized ovum simply because we have granted such a status to the fertilized ovum. The slide into absurdity is thereby avoided.

There are other grounds on which the point of conception constitutes a decisive juncture as well. Signally, there is a crucial difference between a fertilized ovum and its unfertilized counterpart. If we could preserve alive an unfertilized ovum, we would only and always have just that—an unfertilized ovum. However, if we could preserve alive a fertilized ovum, we would eventually witness the emergence of a human being. The fertilized ovum is

---

8. According to data cited by John T. Noonan in his essay "An Almost Absolute Value in History," in *The Morality of Abortion,* ed. John T. Noonan (Cambridge: Harvard University Press, 1970), p. 55.

on a trajectory that will in the course of normal development yield a human being. An unfertilized ovum is on *no* such trajectory, and in that sense it is not a "potential human person" but only a "potential cause of a potential human person." To respect the existence of the fertilized ovum is to respect the unique potential that is built into it, a potential that only needs sustaining nurture for it to be actualized, but this is decidedly not the case with the unfertilized ovum. To draw the line at conception is to recognize this difference and assign it moral significance.

It should be noted that if we assume the existence of an individual-specific divine intention for developing fetal life— namely, that it continue in its normal course of development— we do not thereby automatically settle all the moral dilemmas associated with particular abortions. Individual cases will still present tragic conflicting factors that also ought to be taken into account (viz., it is God's will that those factors at least be considered) in reaching a final determination in the matter. To say there is a divine intention that fetal life be preserved and protected is not to say that it has to be preserved and protected at all costs, without regard to the consequences. It is, however, to suggest that we ought always, even before we begin our analysis of a particular case, to be inclined to preserve and protect fetal life. The assumption that the divine intention for fetal life is individual-specific reorders the abortion debate: it suggests that it is abortion that requires justification and not the preserving of fetal life.

But now, having found some reasonable arguments to support the claim that the fetus does have a strong right to life from conception, we should not lose sight of the fact that this position also entails some substantially problematic features. Indeed, unless we can modify our position we will have to live with implications that carry with them considerable moral tension.

THE GRADUALIST VARIANT OF THE POTENTIALITY PRINCIPLE

There is a theory—I'll call it the gradualist theory—that does serve to modify the right-to-life-from-conception position so as to bring it into accord with the intuitive beliefs of most people. It holds that the right to life gradually becomes stronger as the newly fertilized ovum develops into a newborn infant, that there is no decisive all-or-nothing moment, that just as there is a continuous and gradual line of physical development from conception to birth (and beyond), so there is a continuous and gradual development in the right to life. This means that as the pregnancy progresses the reasons required to justify an abortion have to become increasingly more substantial. It means that using an IUD or a morning-after pill (both of which are presumed to abort zygotes) is not as serious an act as terminating the life of a five- or six-month-old fetus. To use the IUD because one wishes to travel to Europe unencumbered by a pregnancy may be morally problematic, but to terminate a six-month pregnancy for the same reason would be outrageous. Though strictly abortifacient, the IUD strikes most people as being closer in its moral seriousness to contraception than to infanticide, while terminating a pregnancy at six months seems to be closer in its moral seriousness to infanticide. In considering the stages backward from newborn to fetus to embryo to zygote, most people instinctively become increasingly reluctant to recognize a strong right to life, feeling that abortion becomes less and less morally objectionable—and the gradualist theory presents a reasonable basis for supposing that this instinctive reaction may be valid.

We have already noted that the most liberal theories are quick to classify abortion as elective surgery, as no more serious than a piece of cosmetic surgery, and that they are forced to minimize the evil involved in infanticide. The most conservative theories, on the other hand, are quick to classify early abortions as murder—even abortions induced by the IUD and the morning-after pill. Such theories cannot adequately account for the widespread conviction that later abortions are intrinsically more serious than very early abortions. They hold all related acts equally permissible or objectionable, whether killing zygotes, embryos, fetuses, infants, children, or adults. By comparison, the gradualist theory clearly provides a more accurate reflection of what is generally accepted, neither countenancing the lax attitude of the liberal theories toward abortion and infanticide nor capitulating to the severe judgments passed by the conservative theories. It seems to have common moral sense on its side. This is the great strength of a gradualist theory: it best squares with most people's convictions about the full range of abortion cases. Indeed, the gradualist position is simply the systematic working out of two basic convictions: first, that a later abortion is more serious than an earlier one, and second, that killing infants is a serious moral offense, intrinsically objectionable, a violation of a strong claim to life. Though it is not a problem-free theory (I would contend that there are no such theories in the abortion debate), its advantages are nonetheless considerable, and it is well worth trying to work out the theoretical difficulties that confront it.

Proponents of the gradualist theory maintain that the right to life can be a matter of degree, with some individuals having more of a right to life than others. This notion should not strike us as altogether peculiar, for it is not without precedent in other areas. We generally think, for example, that a child's right to self-determination (i.e., the right to make its own moral and prudential decisions as well as to make choices on matters of personal taste) becomes stronger as it grows older. Indeed, we assume that as the child grows toward adulthood, its right to self-determination not only extends into additional areas but becomes stronger; we assume that parents and others have an increasing obligation to honor the child's right to make its own decisions and that considerations that might justify an imposition of parental will on the child at an earlier time may not be sufficient at a later time. Proponents of the gradualist position believe that the right to life similarly increases in strength with the passage of time and the development of the relevant features.

The question we must now address is, of course, how the gradualist position can be reconciled with the premise of an individual-specific divine intention that developing human life be preserved and protected from the point of conception onward. How could it be that killing a zygote would be inherently less morally objectionable than killing an infant if both zygote and infant are objects of an individual-specific divine intention? The answer would have to lie in the contention that different sorts of violations of a given divine intention need not all fall into the same moral category. We can investigate this contention further by considering an analogy.

Suppose that it is my intention, as I place a seed in the ground, that a mature tree ultimately emerge, and that my intention continues as I water the emerging seedling and later trim the young tree. It does not follow that removing the seed from the ground, uprooting the seedling, and chopping down the young tree would be equally objectionable in my eyes, even though each act contravenes, in some general sense, the same intention. This suggests that the category of intention is not incompatible with the notion of degrees of right and wrong. And we might further note that having an original intention for the seed, for the seedling, and for the young tree does not commit us to the view that one is never justified in thwarting the process that has been started. Other considerations might conceivably enter into the situation to require us to remove the tree (seed or seedling). Moreover, it seems reasonable to suppose that circumstances that would justify removing the seed from the ground might not be good enough to justify chopping down the young tree. In other words, increasingly stronger reasons would be needed to justify abandoning my original intention as the tree grew from seed to maturity. In light of this analogy, I think it could be reasonably argued that one can consistently invoke the divine intention as a moral category crucial to the abortion discussion while at the same time seriously entertaining or even adopting the following positions: (1) later abortions are inherently more objectionable than earlier ones, (2) some abortions are morally justified, and (3) stronger reasons are required to justify a later abortion than are required to justify an earlier one.

But which relevant features that the fetus is gradually acquiring might proportionally increase the strength of its claim to life? It could not be personal characteristics or rational abilities, for they are not acquired in the womb. But the fetus *is* progressively and gradually developing the physiological basis for personal life: it is the brain and central nervous system that make possible consciousness as well as rational activity and personal agency. So it might well be argued that the level of the development of the brain and central nervous system is key to a determination of the strength of a right to life. Inasmuch as this process continues after birth, the argument implies that the right to life must continue to gain in strength as postnatal physiological development proceeds. This would entail that an older child or adult would have a stronger right to life than an infant. But this is not problematic if our only concern is that we might jeopardize the infant's standing as the bearer of a serious claim to a right to life, for we can consistently claim that the killing of an infant is a heinous moral offense—its right to life being *that* serious—while still contending that an older child's or adult's right to life may be even stronger than the infant's. In fact I think most of us tend to feel that something like this is the case. For instance, we may very well feel a stronger obligation to save the life of an adult (or older child) than to save the life of an infant should we be in the unfortunate and tragic circumstances of having to choose between them. Nor do I think that this inclination is merely a product of our awareness that the adult (or child) is already an intimate part of a matrix of human relationships and would be more sorely missed; to some considerable extent, I think, we make the decision because we implicitly discern the presence of personal life in the child (and adult) and its absence in the infant.

So the gradualist variant of the potentiality principle that we are discussing here has a number of interesting implications. It dictates that newborn infants have a strong right to life—killing infants is seriously wrong, a grave evil—and that as a fetus moves forward from the point of conception its right to life increases in strength until it becomes a person, *at which point considerations of degree no longer apply,* since once one is a full-fledged person, it is not possible to become more of a person. It is, of course, possible to become a more intelligent person or a better person, but that does not make one more of a person. We would not want to propose that people have a stronger right to life as adults than they have as teenagers or that an Einstein would have a stronger right to life than a person of average intelligence. But there would be two periods in human development when considerations of degree would be applicable. The first would be that period (mostly fetal but also neonatal) during which the physiological basis for personal life is developing, especially the brain and central nervous system. Beginning with conception and ending with the start of the emergence of personal life, the strength of the right to life could be measured primarily by the extent of brain development. The second period would comprise the time of transition during which the infant is acquiring personal characteristics but is still subpersonal. During this period the strength of the right to life could perhaps be best measured by the degree to which those personal characteristics have been acquired.

If our duty to respect developing fetal life is the product of some nonmoral property, as this theory suggests, then to the extent that the fetus has this property, the rest of us will have the duty to respect its life. Clearly, this property must be one that admits of degrees—and "potentiality" in the sense that we are using it in this context (i.e., to indicate an inherent capacity to develop into a person) does not admit of degrees. A full-term infant, a six-month-old fetus, and a newly fertilized ovum all possess the same potentiality for personhood; none possesses it less and none possesses it more. So the nonmoral property that serves as a gauge of the *increasing* strength of a fetus's claim to life cannot be a potentiality for personhood. A better candidate is the biological basis for the subsequent realization of personhood, a variable that can be assessed as a matter of degree: the zygote has very little of this, the six-month-old fetus with its developing brain has much more, and the full-term infant even more. Nor need we fear that emphasizing the biological maturation of the fetus as the crucial nonmoral property would in any way entail abandoning the concept of potentiality, for where no natural potential for personhood exists, no special status can exist either. Indeed, from the moment of conception there is a natural potential for a unique organism to develop that will in time be able to provide the biological basis for a personal being. Such potentiality merits the respect that has traditionally been captured by talk of a right to life. The gradualist theory simply adds the further claim that as the unique *biological* potential unfolds and takes shape, this claim to life must be increasingly respected.

PROBLEMS WITH THE GRADUALIST THEORY

Philip Devine has raised a number of objections to the gradualist theory. By confronting these problems we can perhaps get a clearer picture of the gradualist theory itself.

1. Devine's First Criticism

If personhood or humanity admits of degrees before birth, then it would seem it must admit of degrees after birth as well.... But few hold and fewer still teach that a ten-year-old child can be killed on lighter grounds than an adult.[9]

This is not a valid criticism of the gradualist position as I have outlined it, since that position dictates that although the right to life is indeed a matter of degree both before and after birth, once one becomes a person, considerations of degree no longer apply: a ten-year-old child is presumed to be a person with as strong a right to life as any adult's.

---

9. Devine, pp. 79–80.

Even if Devine's first criticism is not entirely to the point, however, it does serve to raise a problematic question that proponents of the gradualist position must face: at what point in human development does there come into existence a person about whom we can dismiss as inapplicable talk of degrees when speaking of the right to life or the intrinsic evil of killing the innocent? We might tentatively note that personhood is emerging at least as early as the second year, when the child begins to articulate words and phrases. Importantly, as the child "acquires language his parents are able to use words to describe him and his actions, and he begins to build into his self-concept more differentiated aspects of his 'goodness,' 'badness,' 'cuteness,' and 'boyness.' All of these are important in developing his concept of himself in relation to the world he lives in."[10] So by the end of the second year a rudimentary awareness of personal identity is evolving. This process accelerates during the third year, when the child "shows a positive propensity to understand his environment and to comply with cultural demands. He is no longer a mere infant."[11] By the end of this period there is a self-conscious being with a sense of a self enduring through time, capable of exercising agency and engaging in rudimentary rational activity. It is, in other words, a person. To be sure, this person stands in need of much growth and development, but nonetheless it is a person and therefore an individual with a maximal claim to life. After this point in the development of the individual, proponents of the gradualist position need no longer speak of the right to life or the intrinsic wrongness of killing as having degrees.

As we have already noted, the gradualist position dictates that considerations of degree apply only (1) during the period of fetal development and (2) during that postnatal period when personal life is beginning to emerge. The latter specification may give many people a little pause, but it need not prove to be seriously objectionable as long as proponents of the position acknowledge a *strong* claim to a right to life from birth. Indeed, by the time of birth, the infant's claim to a right to life is so strong and the occasions for a serious conflict of rights so rare (unlike the situation of the fetus, in which complications—in-

---

10. Wilbert James McKeachie and Charlotte Lackner Doyle, *Psychology* (Reading, Mass.: Addison-Wesley, 1966), p. 461.

11. Arnold Gesell and Frances Ilg, *Infant and Child in the Culture of Today* (New York: Harper, 1943), p. 63.

volving, for example, the life of the mother vs. the life of the fetus—are much more common) that talk of degrees of a right to life has no real practical import. Nevertheless, *in theory* proponents of the gradualist position are committed to saying that taking the life of a young child in whom personhood is beginning to emerge is more serious than taking the life of an infant in whom personhood has not yet begun to emerge.

I don't think most people would consider this implication of the gradualist position to be intolerable as long as it were maintained that the newborn infant has a very strong claim to life, that *all* such acts of homicide are morally outrageous, serious violations of a right to life, whether the individual killed is an infant, a young or older child, or an adult. If faced with having to choose between saving the life of a ten-year-old or the life of an infant, I think many people would instinctively feel a stronger claim on the part of the ten-year-old. Similarly, I think many people would feel that an infant with personhood emerging has a stronger claim upon our lifesaving efforts than does a newborn infant devoid of personal characteristics. Far from providing counterexamples to the gradualist theory, these considerations seem to provide support for it. And in looking at difficulties that attach to a given theory we must always do so in the context of a comparison with those difficulties that attach to alternative theories: which are more problematic? The case can be made, I think, that the implications of the gradualist theory are easier to live with than the implications of either the standard conservative theory (e.g., that the use of the IUD is as seriously wrong as ending a seven-month pregnancy or killing a ten-year-old child under comparable circumstances) or certain liberal theories (e.g., that abortion and infanticide are intrinsically matters of little or no moral consequence).

2. Devine's Second Criticism

It has ... been argued that a graduation from personhood into nonpersonhood can be observed at the end of life.... What the analogy with abortion leads to is the killing of old people (1) without their consent and (2) for the sake of relieving others of the burden they pose.[12]

---

12. Devine, p. 80.

If this is in fact an implication of the gradualist theory, then it is beyond question a monstrous one, providing strong ground for rejecting the theory itself. But in defense of the theory it could surely be argued that although there is a gradual decline at the end of life from personhood into nonpersonhood and with it a reduction in the strength of one's right to life, it does not carry with it the damaging implications that Devine suggests. For as long as there is personal life present in the individual, even if the individual is fading in and out of consciousness or having alternating periods of lucidity and incoherence, still the individual remains a person with a person's strong right to life. Killing would be murder in such circumstances. To be sure, in the course of aging, persons may become senile, their mental deterioration progressing to the point where they revert to a childlike existence. This may indeed be tragic, but it does not alter the fact that, like children, those who are childlike are persons who have a person's right to life; nothing in the developmental theory necessitates a denial of this. The senile may become burdensome and socially useless, but no proponent of the gradualist position need hold that that consideration either justifies or excuses an act of murder, which is what killing "childlike" old people would be.

But what about the transition period when an aging person might degenerate even further from childlike senility to subpersonal existence? Are we licensed to kill in such circumstances, either during the transition period itself or when a permanent subpersonal state is reached? The gradualist position indicates that we cannot, for to kill individuals who are in the transition period, in which there are glimmerings of personal life, would be to take the life of an individual who has a right to life even if the strength of that right is less than that of a full-fledged person. After all, it does not follow from the fact that some individuals have a *weaker* right to life than others that they have a *weak* right. We ought not to kill such individuals merely because they are burdensome or socially useless, because they continue to have a right to life that is still strong enough to override such considerations, and that right to life must be honored.

Individuals whose senility reaches the point at which they are conscious but nevertheless *permanently* subpersonal constitute a different category. It is the potentiality principle, however, not the gradualist position that commits us to the view that the permanently subpersonal no longer have a right to life. But it could well be argued that such cases ought to be handled in the same way we handle cases of individuals so severely retarded that they never will achieve personhood: earlier in this chapter we invoked Philip Devine's "overflow principle" with respect to such individuals—the principle that respect for persons spills over to what is and has been intimately connected with persons. There seems no good reason why a proponent of the gradualist position should not likewise invoke the overflow principle in this context to neutralize—curiously—an objection that Devine himself raises. For even if one characterizes a subpersonally senile individual as a badly deteriorated human organism that once supported personal life but is now only able to support a less than personal consciousness, one can nevertheless grant that the individual is a vehicle through which personal life was manifested at one time and for which ongoing respect is therefore appropriate—respect, that is, in the form of care, the provision of small pleasures, the giving of relief from suffering, and so on.

Another important consideration in this matter is the fact that in actual practice there is a grave moral risk in acting on the assumption that a severely senile individual is no longer a person. Such individuals are quite unlike fetuses in that we may well be quite uncertain over the extent of their inner personal life; overt behavior cannot serve as an infallible guide in making such a determination. Additionally, whereas in the case of abortion there is a conflict between the woman's right to determine what happens in and to her own body and the fetus's right to life, there is no comparable conflict in the case of the subpersonally senile that might override their claim to respect. On the basis of all these considerations, I think it reasonable to conclude that the developmental theory does not commit us to killing the senile for convenience' sake as Devine suggests.

3. Devine's Third Criticism

What we are looking for is a way of making abortion decisions that offer some hope of rational agreement. And there seems to be no stable, nonarbitrary way of correlating stages of fetal development with justifying grounds.[13]

---

13. Devine, p. 78.

The implication of this criticism is that the gradualist theory only serves to tell us that later abortions are more serious affairs than earlier abortions and that we have to have proportionally better reasons to justify them, but that it does not tell us how good those reasons have to be at any given point of fetal development, and so in this regard it is less helpful than decisive moment theories that give very definite advice. Certainly a position that assumes a full and unqualified right to life from conception prescribes a clear moral injunction: all abortions are morally wrong, with the possible exception of cases in which the life of the mother is at stake. The position that presumes that the right to life begins at the point of viability dictates that before the fetus reaches that point one is justified in having an abortion if it is in one's self-interest to do so, but that it would be morally wrong to abort the fetus after it has attained viability. Both of these theories provide specific counsel, whereas the gradualist theory continues to leave things pretty much up in the air. All the counsel it has to give is that better reasons are required for later abortions than for earlier ones.

One answer to this criticism is that general advice is better than bad advice. It may indeed be that the right-to-life-from-conception position provides very specific direction on abortion issues—but it does so at a cost that many are not willing to pay. It entails that the use of the IUD is as seriously wrong as an abortion at seven months, that zygotes that would otherwise perish as the result of spontaneous (natural) abortions have the same claim to our lifesaving efforts that perishing adult human beings have! The clear-cut implication of the viability theory that only the mother's interests are relevant to an abortion decision likewise carries with it a high price for its simple answers: first, we must accept the view that the fetus has no value that can override any interests that the woman might have (no matter how trivial). I think it fair to say that the capacity of a moral theory on abortion to generate concrete advice is a virtue *all else being equal,* but in this case all else does not seem to be equal.

Advocates of the gradualist theory would do well at this point to begin to rank in seriousness the kind of reasons people give when seeking an abortion and then proceed to determine (with the help of expert advice) critical junctures in fetal development. It is within *that* context that individual abortion decisions will have to be made. It is doubtful that such decisions could ever be made with any kind of precision: a great deal of struggle and agony would almost inevitably be involved in such deliberations (assuming one approached them with moral seriousness and not simply a self-serving attitude). But I think much moral decision making is like this in any case. We may believe, to take but one example, that promises ought to be kept scrupulously, but we may also believe (rightly) that the consequences either for oneself or others of keeping a given promise could become sufficiently disastrous so as to relieve us of our obligation to keep it. That being the case, we may well wonder when consequences will have become sufficiently negative for us to say we have reached that point? No formulas are available to make such a determination; one simply struggles with this kind of moral question. This is characteristic of much of the moral life, and there is no reason to believe that honest and careful reflection on the abortion issue must yield a theory that is able to crank out precise answers to all abortion questions.

7

⟡The Species
Principle

When we take the potentiality principle (namely, that only persons and potential persons have a right to life) and augment it with the overflow principle (namely, that what is intimately associated with persons deserves a special but subordinate respect), we come very close to having what amounts to a species principle. But not quite. For the species principle gives to *all* members of the human species the same strong right to life. It recognizes no "second class citizens" (e.g., the severely retarded) covered by an overflow principle but instead holds that all human life (including the severely retarded) is *equally* inviolable by virtue of membership in the species Homo sapiens. It is not by possessing personal characteristics or by possessing the potential for such characteristics that individuals attain a status that merits the special respect we associate with the right to life, say the proponents of the species principle; it is sufficient simply that one is a member of the human species. In this, then, there is an explicit *rejection* of the doctrine that an individual Homo sapiens has its special status because it is either a person or a potential person.

Presumably, however, the species principle would have to be interpreted as maintaining that only members of the human species who are conscious or have a potential for consciousness have a right to life. Otherwise the irreversibly comatose, who are still members of the human species but have no prospect for conscious existence, would have a right to life, and this would be an odd implication to have to accept. With this qualification, the species principle dictates the following conclusions:

Have a right to life:	Do not have a right to life:
fetuses	irreversibly comatose
infants	
children	
adults	
reversibly comatose	
severely retarded	
less severely retarded	

One advocate of the species principle has claimed that it is the standard view and that philosophers and theologians who disagree with it are in essence dissenting from the moral conscience of the larger community by their invention and introduction of the actuality and potentiality principles.[1] And indeed the strength of the species principle is that it accounts very well for what most people seem to believe—namely, that infants (who are not yet persons in the strict sense of the term), adult humans (who undeniably are persons), and grossly retarded humans (who never will be persons) all possess the same special dignity and value. Essentially, the one thing they have in common is that they are all Homo sapiens. In contrast, nonhuman animals, according to standard belief, do not have a right to life despite the fact that their intelligence may be superior to that of severely retarded humans. The only way to account for this is in terms of the species principle, say its proponents.

DEFINING "HUMAN SPECIES"

But how do we define "member of the human species"? First of all, we can offer the following straightforward definition: a member of the human species is any individual conceived by human parents, which is to say that membership in the human species begins at that moment when the human ovum is fertil-

---

1. See Roger Wertheimer, "Philosophy on Humanity," *Abortion: New Directions for Policy Studies*, ed. Edward Manier et al. (South Bend, Ind.: University of Notre Dame Press, 1977), pp. 118-19.

ized by the male sperm.[2] Such a view has the advantage of being decisive and clear-cut in specifying precisely who has a right to life, but it also inherits the difficulties associated with the theory that assumes a full right to life from conception.

A more ambiguous understanding of "member of the human species" has been offered by Roger Wertheimer, who contends that there is no set of necessary and sufficient conditions for being a member of the human species.[3] No definition, he argues, will prove successful. "Conceived of human parents" won't do because it excludes the first members of the species (it would entail that Adam and Eve were not members of the human species) and because it includes terata, grossly deformed genetic monstrosities. And certainly matters *are* ambiguous when it comes to classifying human fetuses. While a human infant is clearly a member of the human species, there is something odd about classifying a zygote as a Homo sapiens—and that of course opens the door to uncertainty in classifying fetal life as development proceeds from zygote to infant. But the fact that the species principle does not always have precise implications in such matters need not be construed as a fatal flaw. On the contrary, the fact that the implications of the species principle are ambiguous in a situation in which we are also uncertain about the moral status of a particular individual could be counted a mark in its favor. At least in this regard the species principle and our intuitions are consistent.

TWO VERSIONS OF THE SPECIES PRINCIPLE

Despite the points that recommend it, however, the species principle has come under severe attack on the grounds that it is analogous to racism.[4] Just as the racist holds that the members of a given race ought to be treated specially for no reason other than that they belong to that race, so the proponent of the species principle holds that Homo sapiens ought to be treated specially (viz., they ought to be presumed to have a right to life)

---

2. This definition is suggested by John T. Noonan in his essay "An Almost Absolute Value in History," in *The Morality of Abortion*, ed. John T. Noonan (Cambridge: Harvard University Press, 1970), p. 51.

3. Wertheimer, pp. 123–24.

4. See, for example, Jonathan Glover, *Causing Death and Saving Lives* (New York: Penguin Books, 1977), p. 50.

for no reason other than that they are Homo sapiens. In order to refute such charges, proponents of the species principle would have to demonstrate that there are in fact some relevant differences between the species that justify their discrimination. Let us consider two such lines of defense.

Version One: Homo sapiens as Bearers of the Divine Image

It can be argued that being a member of the human species endows one with a right to life because it is that species in which persons or divine image bearers are found. Granted, some defective members of the human species have no potential whatsoever for rational, moral, or spiritual agency, but that fact does not affect their status, because what is crucial is the fact that they belong to the same species as those who *can* exercise such agency. Indeed, to determine who possesses a right to life we need not inquire into an individual's own rational, moral, or spiritual capacities; we need only determine the species to which the individual belongs. And it is the species Homo sapiens alone that endows its members with a right to life, because it is only in that species that persons can be found.

The concept of the image of God can be introduced in either of two ways, depending on how we formulate this version of the species principle. Defining *divine image bearers* to mean "one who reflects the divine nature by virtue of his or her capacity, whether potential or actualized, to exercise rational, moral, and spiritual agency," we could argue that the presence of divine image bearers sanctifies the whole human species and that the species in turn endows its members with a right to life. This would allow us to say that not all holders of the right to life are image bearers—that a congenital idiot, for example, is a member of the human species and therefore has a right to life but that since it has no prospect for personal life it is not in the image of God. However, this is not the only way to put matters. We could also argue that the presence of *persons* (i.e., those who possess an actualized or potential capacity for rational, moral, and spiritual agency) sanctifies the human species, which in turn endows all its members with a right to life—which is to say, it renders them in the image of God. According to this formulation, all members of the human species would be in the image of God, not just those with a rational capacity: congenital idiots would have as strong a right to life as any other human beings because they too are members of the human species and therefore in the image of God.

But however the principle is formulated, the logic involved is the same: there are individual members of the species Homo sapiens who are rational agents and because of that fact this particular species endows *all* its members with a right to life regardless of whether the individual member shares in that capacity or even has a potential for it. In being asked to endorse the species principle in this form, we are being asked to believe that Homo sapiens are morally special because of the presence of personal life in the species in general, while individual Homo sapiens in whom this personal life is totally absent are not rendered "unspecial," nor is their moral status in any way qualified or jeopardized by this absence. This argument clearly implies that if there were no personal beings in the human species, then the human species would *not* be special at all—an implication that advocates of the species principle fully accept.

There is no formal contradiction in the claim being made by the species principle, but there is something odd about it nonetheless—something that I would suggest is contrary to common procedure. Surely it is not typical to conclude that a normal adult human being has a special status or a right to life on the basis of the fact that *others* in the species are persons, their existence somehow sanctifying the species, which in turn endows the individual with his or her special status. Everyday reasoning is not so convoluted. Rather, we move directly from the fact that a given individual is a person to the conclusion that this individual has a right to life. The relevance of the appeal to Homo sapiens is that it is a central consideration in determining who is or is not a person or a potential person.

It may be surmised that our inclination to assume that all Homo sapiens ought to be accorded a right to life is really a product of our tendency to think of all Homo sapiens as *normal* Homo sapiens. It seems to me that when we think of Homo sapiens in general we do not ordinarily give any real thought to the atypical and relatively rare cases of those who have no potential for personal life (e.g., the congenital idiot)—and when we do specifically reflect on such individuals, I think most of us tend to experience some puzzlement over their exact moral status.

The logic of the species principle is, however, not peculiar to the species principle, and perhaps we can understand it more clearly if we take a look at the similar logic of rule utilitarianism, a moral theory that has been widely adopted by moral philosophers. It is interesting that while rule utilitarianism has been widely respected, endorsed, and defended, the species principle, which shares the same basic logic, finds few advocates and is even the object of considerable scorn. Rule utilitarianism has in part found favor because it provides a utilitarian alternative to act utilitarianism, which is widely perceived to be marred by moral flaws. Indeed, act utilitarianism, though never completely bereft of able advocates, has recently been very much a beleaguered minority position. Yet the logic of the actuality principle and also of the potentiality principle is similar to that of the less favored act utilitarianism.

Act utilitarianism dictates that we ought to perform those acts that will maximize overall human happiness, that we must evaluate individual acts to determine whether they have the property of maximizing happiness. (More precisely, act utilitarianism affirms that a moral agent should perform an act if there is no alternative act that will produce more net happiness.) If a given act will serve to maximize happiness, then according to act utilitarianism, we are obliged to perform it. In other words, we are obliged to apply the principle of utility ("Maximize the happiness to the greatest number") on an act-by-act basis. Similarly, the actuality and potentiality principles dictate that the crucial criterion (viz., the presence of personhood or a natural potential for personhood) ought to be applied on an individual-by-individual basis: if the individual human organism possesses the relevant property, it should be assumed that it enjoys a full moral standing; if not, it can be assumed that it lacks that standing.

But many people contend that an act-by-act application of the principle of utility turns out to have unacceptably unsettling implications. For instance, it sanctions individual acts of punishing the innocent, telling lies, failing to repay debts, and so on, all in circumstances in which most people would judge such acts to be wrong, even outrageously wrong. That is to say, act utilitarianism is widely held to conflict with common moral sense. There is another version of utilitarianism—rule utilitarianism— that avoids these moral pitfalls by using the principle of utility to determine what secondary moral rules ought to be adopted instead of seeking to assess individual acts themselves. These secondary rules can then be used to determine which acts we should perform and which we should not. Thus, according to rule utilitarianism we don't ask "Will this act of lying, this act of stealing, or this act of punishing an innocent person maximize overall happiness?" but rather, "Is this act of lying, stealing, or punishing the innocent prohibited by a relevant moral rule?" If the principle of utility dictates that we should adopt rules against lying, stealing, and punishing the innocent, then the proponent of rule utilitarianism would say that we should not perform such acts even on occasions when doing so would maximize happiness. It is rules, not acts, that we must judge by reference to the principle of utility, says the rule utilitarian, and we should adopt those rules that will do more to maximize happiness than any other alternative rules.

As I said, the logic of the species principle is similar to the logic of rule utilitarianism. Briefly, just as the rule utilitarian uses the crucial property of maximizing happiness to select rules that in turn determine which acts are obligatory even if some of those acts do not themselves maximize happiness, so the advocate of the species principle uses the crucial property of personhood to select the species that in turn determines who possess a right to life even though some of those whom the principle includes among those who have a right to life are not themselves persons, actually or potentially.[5]

I am not a utilitarian, and so I don't have to choose between act utilitarianism and rule utilitarianism; but if I were a utilitarian, I would have serious reservations about the rule utilitarian strategy, even though I might be eager to avoid the awkward moral implications of act utilitarianism. For it does seem odd, even contradictory perhaps, that I should be committed as a utilitarian to maximizing human happiness and at the same time be obliged as a rule utilitarian to refrain from acts that will maximize happiness—obliged to refrain simply because such acts breach a secondary rule. Why, *as a utilitarian*, should I honor a moral rule that in a given set of circumstances prevents me from maximizing happiness? And yet that is exactly what I am obliged to do if I attempt to avoid the embarrassing implications of act utilitarianism by turning to rule utilitarianism.

The unease I would experience were I a rule utilitarian in abandoning the fundamental utilitarian commitment to maxi-

---

5. In both instances, more formally put, the shared logic is as follows: category C, by virtue of property P, endows members M of C with special status S, and this is so whether or not M itself possesses P.